Stories for the Mind and Soul

An ESL Prose Reader/Worktext

Theresa Mezo
Rosa A. Vallejo

Inter American University, Metropolitan Campus

International Thomson Editores
An International Thomson Publishing Company I**T**P

Mexico • Albany • Bonn • Boston • Johannesburg • London • Madrid • Melbourne
New York • Paris • San Francisco • San Juan, PR • Santiago • São Paulo • Singapore • Tokyo
Toronto • Washington

Stories for the Mind and Soul

ISBN 968-7529-53-9

© 1999 by International Thomson Editores, S.A. de C.V.

I⍿P International Thomson Editores, S.A. de C.V. is an *International Thomson Publishing company*. The ITP logo is a registered trademark used herein under license.

Mexico and Central America
Phone. (525)281-2906
Fax (525)281-2656
Seneca 53, Col. Polanco
E-mail: clientes@mail.internet.com.mx
Mexico, D.F. 11560 MEXICO

South America
Phone/Fax (562)524-4688
E-mail: ldevore@ibm.net
Santiago, CHILE

Phone/Fax (541)777-0960
E-mail:sdeluque@ba.net
Buenos Aires, ARGENTINA

Puerto Rico and the Caribbean
Phone. (787)758-7580
Fax(787)758-7573
E-mail:102154.1127@compuserve.com
Hato Rey, PUERTO RICO

Spain
Phone. (3491)446-3350
Fax (3491)446-6218
E-mail: itesparaninfo.pedidos@mad.servicom.es
Madrid, SPAIN

Brazil
Phone/Fax (5511)211-4743
E-mail: thomson@dialdata.com.br
São Paulo, BRAZIL

Development Editor: Lenore Cohen
Director, ELT: Francisco Lozano
Editorial and Production Director: Miguel Ángel Toledo Castellanos
Proofreading: Philip Daniels
Cover Design and Composition: X-Libris
Illustrations: Claudia Navarro

987654321   9XI8

Printed in Mexico

Contents

Preface

Stories for the Mind and Soul is an ESL prose reader that can be used at basic or intermediate levels depending on the language proficiency standards established by the institution. The main goal of this book is to develop reading, writing, and oral fluency skills. The authors have written stories that cover appealing and diverse topics with the belief that these will motivate students to become active readers. Because research shows that working collaboratively is important for the development of logical reasoning skills, we have created a variety of interactive tasks to be performed in dyads, small groups or as whole classroom discussion. The majority of the activities can be done either in writing or orally.

The textbook encourages students to construct meaning by responding to the text as well as through the development of reading strategies to help them in problem solving. Students will read critically and contrast their particular views with those presented in the narratives. The Response Journal Questions allow students to express their reactions to the story and to construct meaning by bringing the text to their own personal experience. Sharing their answers to these questions will allow students to understand that readers can have different responses to a text and that each of these responses has value. Through discussion they can then arrive at more complex responses. The mapping exercises will allow students to establish the elements that make up the structure of the narrative. Pre- and post–reading activities will help students develop reading strategies to help them become more efficient readers.

The stories and activities in *Stories for the Mind and Soul* promote a student-centered classroom in which ESL students can work in a non-threatening environment and feel comfortable enough to express their views, make inferences, arrive at conclusions and debate answers orally.

Our students have made us aware that the classroom experience should be a shared one where their views are respected and valued. They have been the source of motivation for this book. We have created the stories and activities in *Stories for the Mind and Soul* in our desire to fulfill these needs.

Biographies

Theresa Mezo was born in Fajardo, Puerto Rico. She has a B.A. in English Education from the University of Puerto Rico and an M.A. in TESOL from New York University. While in New York, she taught ESL to Russian immigrants and Asian students, and worked in a Ceta-Program for Latin Americans. She has taught at different campuses of the University of Puerto Rico and the Inter American University. She has been teaching ESL, literature, and writing courses at the IAU Metro Campus for thirteen years.

Rosa A. Vallejo was born in San Lorenzo, Puerto Rico, and grew up in New York City. She has an M.A. in TESOL from the Inter American University of Puerto Rico and is a Ph.D. candidate in English at Indiana University of Pennsylvania. She has been affiliated with the Inter American University for ten years, and teaches English communication skills, literature, and writing courses to ESL and English dominant students.

To the Teacher

Stories for the Mind and Soul presents original stories with themes that address current issues of interest to our students. We have created activities for these stories in which meaningful communication is encouraged through collaboration in a student-centered classroom. The students' responses to these stories are an important element in this communication. They will come to understand that their responses are valued and respected, and are also an integral part of the learning process. Furthermore, these activities will allow them to develop reading strategies to help them become more efficient readers.

The book provides a Response Journal Questionnaire for students to respond to each story. Students should be encouraged to answer these questions immediately after reading. These questions will later be used in classroom discussions at a time set aside by you. The book also provides a chart for mapping each story. This activity will help students become better acquainted with the elements of the story. Comprehension questions are included for better understanding of the text. Finally, the activities in the Springboard section will encourage students to analyze and discuss the issues presented and to go beyond the boundaries of the story.

In the *Content and Scope* chart you will find the main focus of each story and other issues related to that focus. You will also find the overall idea of the skills covered in the activities presented.

We have not included specific vocabulary exercises in this book because we believe that the students' vocabulary needs are individual. We think that collaborative activities in which students share their knowledge of vocabulary will generate interest and participation on the students' part. The Vocabulary Builder on pages 163-164 provides a space for students to develop their own individual glossary.

In groups, students may exchange and clarify their understanding of the words they have selected from each reading. These words can then be shared in whole class discussions during which you can clarify any misconceptions. From our own experience, we have found that having some class time set aside for this type of collaborative activity is especially effective. You can ask the students to select and find the definition of at least two words from each selection. They can then write a sentence with each word. During collaborative vocabulary activities, students will be able to share what they have learned with their classmates. We also believe it is important to emphasize what students know rather than what they do not know. One way to do this is for you to ask the students to underline the vocabulary they do understand in a selected paragraph. They will be surprised to see that they have a greater wealth of vocabulary than they believed. The words they do not underline can be used in collaborative activities. Of course, we believe that before students reach for the dictionary they should use techniques such as context clues, word parts and cognates to arrive at meaning.

It is our hope that *Stories for the Mind and Soul* will result in an innovative and productive experience for you and your students.

To the Student

The stories in this book were primarily written to be read and enjoyed. The first time you read each story, read it all the way through for enjoyment.

Then read the story again to work with the activities your teacher has selected. The Response Journal Questions in the book give you the opportunity to express your reactions to the stories you will read. Your answers to these questions will become an important part of classroom discussion. The other activities in the book are intended to guide you in your interaction with the stories and to help you solve any problems that you might encounter while reading.

In this book you will not find specific vocabulary exercises. We understand that you have a wealth of vocabulary knowledge already. Therefore, you can draw on this knowledge to discover the meaning of the words you do not know. There are several ways you can do this:

- If you come across a word you do not know, continue reading.
  Usually one word will not stop you from understanding the passage you are reading. Later you may want to look up the word.
- Sometimes you will be able to determine the meaning of a word by the words that surround it.
- Looking at the parts of the word can also help you figure out its meaning.
- Determining if a word is a cognate—a word that is written the same way or similarly to one in your language—may help you arrive at the meaning of a word.
- When you cannot arrive at the meaning of the word by using these techniques, you can always use a dictionary.
- You can develop your own glossary by using the Vocabulary Builder on pages 163 and 164.

We hope that your interaction with *Stories for the Mind and Soul* will be an enjoyable and productive experience.

Acknowledgments

Special thanks TO OUR CHILDREN, Viviana, Ariana, Melissa, Aileem, Carin, Liana and Javier, who truly believe our stories have a special message that should be sha ed with the world, and to our extended families, who also inspire us.

For their invaluable assistance:
Prof. Carmen Vélez, IAU Metropolitan Campus
Prof. Lydia Rivera, IAU Metropolitan Campus
Prof. Catherine Toro, UPR Bayamón Campus\English Department
Prof. Lucy Sandoval
Prof. Mildred Lockwood, UPR Río Piedras\General Studies
Prof. Mildred Santiago, UPR Bayamón\ English Department
The Inter American University Writing Circle
Michael Rabell, International Thomson Publishing
Dr. Dalia Rodríguez Aponte, IAU Dean, Humanistic Division
Lcdo. José D. Camacho
Jack Lee Mezo
Dr. Jesús González
Miguel Angel Toledo, Editorial Director, International Thomson Editores
Francisco Lozano, Editor, International Thomson Editores
MDS Marcano Digital Studio

1. Life Rhythms

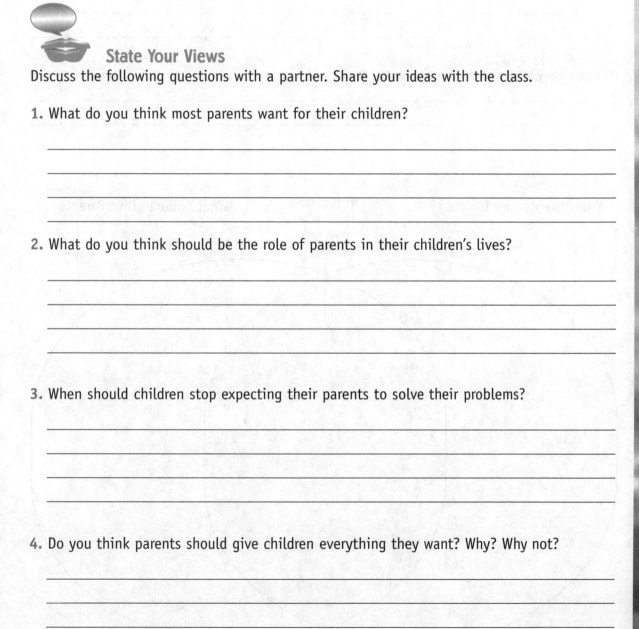

State Your Views

Discuss the following questions with a partner. Share your ideas with the class.

1. What do you think most parents want for their children?

_____
_____
_____
_____

2. What do you think should be the role of parents in their children's lives?

_____
_____
_____
_____

3. When should children stop expecting their parents to solve their problems?

_____
_____
_____
_____

4. Do you think parents should give children everything they want? Why? Why not?

_____
_____
_____
_____

Take a Stand

In groups, share your ideas about the following questions. After your discussion, fill in the chart with those points that the group decides are most important and present them to the class.

1. What do parents owe their children?

_____

_____

_____

2. What do children owe their parents?

_____

_____

_____

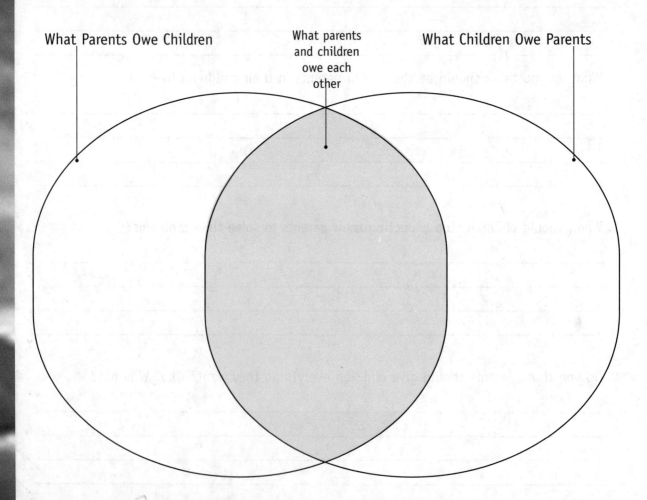

What Parents Owe Children

What parents and children owe each other

What Children Owe Parents

Life Rhythms

Rosa A. Vallejo

Martha hung up the phone. It was a relief to finally disengage herself from the conversation with her sister. She wondered what gave others the right to preach, especially those who had never experienced problems with their own children.

She heard the baby's soft cry begin behind the closed door of her daughter's room and quickly made her way there. She didn't want Laura to wake up. Walking on tiptoe, she crossed over to the white crib and picked up her five-day-old granddaughter. She quickly popped a pacifier in the baby's mouth in order to appease her. As the child calmed down and quieted, she could hear the rhythm of her daughter's breathing. Her daughter lay asleep in a fetal position. The sounds of her breathing came softly and gently through her partially opened mouth.

When Laura had been very young, she had sucked her thumb. Now her arms were crossed over her chest, her exposed hand holding on to her exposed shoulder as if she were embracing herself. She had taught herself to sleep in this position when she was seven and had finally made up her mind to break herself of her thumb-sucking habit. It had taken several months, but she had succeeded in freeing herself from her thumb. Martha had admired Laura's determination and tenacity then, but later she had come to curse these qualities in her daughter. The baby in her arms began to whimper again, and she quickly left the room.

Martha had not known she was to be a grandmother until the day her daughter went into labor. She had received the call just as she was about to go out for dinner.

"Mom?"

At the sound of her daughter's voice all the confusing emotions their relationship triggered in her had rushed through her again. Happiness and apprehension both washed over her.

"Laura, are you all right? What's wrong? You don't sound well."

"Mom, I need you. Can you come to the hospital? You're about to become a grandmother."

She experienced again the feeling of dread that had made her go cold all over when she had heard those words. She wished that she could experience the excitement and joy that a first grandchild is supposed to create. Instead, she felt as apprehensive and confused now as she had when Laura had called. Her old fears had resurfaced and she could not shake them. Was she to live with her daughter's tyranny again? She looked down at the baby and instantly felt ashamed and guilty. She pressed the baby closer, in an attempt to lessen her feelings of guilt.

When Laura was a baby Martha had envisioned her in adolescence, going to parties and bringing home tons of friends. She had imagined a house full of laughter, music and dancing. She had looked beyond the years and imagined her daughter as a happy, self-assured, and successful young woman, enjoying an independent life. But Laura had chosen another path for herself, and instead of sharing those carefree and happy moments, they had spent her daughter's adolescence in the offices of various therapists. Instead of that lovely, carefree young woman, Laura had become a tyrant. From the time her daughter was thirteen, Martha had been dealing with her numerous acts of rebellion.

She had lived through the many embarrassing confrontations with school officials about her daughter's truancy, the binge drinking and the horror of having Laura brought home drunk by a police officer, and the sleepless nights waiting to hear the key turn in the door. How many times had she been on the verge of declaring her missing when Laura would finally appear in the middle of the afternoon and stumble into her room to sleep for twenty-four hours? She shuddered as she thought of it. And all the time Martha had been aware that she was the one considered at fault. The finger was pointed at her, indicting her as a poor example of a parent. They overlooked her involvement in library and PTA programs with her young daughter. They did not consider how she struggled to get Laura to AA meetings or to her therapist.

Laura was determined to do what she wanted to do. When medication was prescribed, she had refused to take it.

"I will not give others control over me," she would declare. "I'm not as crazy as that."

Martha could not understand Laura's anger. She had always been loved. She had never been mistreated. Their lives had been relatively good ones. She tried to appease Laura. She took her shopping, they went on a short vacation, she indulged her in her passion for fast food. Although she seemed to take pleasure in these things and seemed happy and at peace with herself for a while, in the end Laura did what she wanted to do without thinking of the consequences to herself or anyone else.

On the very day that she turned eighteen, Laura declared herself independent and left home for good. At first Martha was stunned, but gradually she began to experience a feeling of relief. She began to sleep through the night, even when she did not hear from Laura for months. During those months alone, she would sometimes question these feelings. But she felt as if her daughter had loosened her hold on her. She knew that nothing would ever stop her from loving her daughter, and deep inside she did miss her, but she had come to understand that she also feared her. She feared Laura's ability to create havoc in her life and her ability to manipulate her. Martha cringed when she saw the role she had assigned to herself. She had tried to fulfill the role of the mother she had always been told she should be. She had done everything in her power in order to try to make Laura happy, no matter the cost to herself. But she came to realize that she had been given an opportunity to reclaim herself and her life, and she made a promise to herself. Never again would she compromise her life or her needs, not even for her daughter.

It had been almost a year since Martha had made that promise. And now her daughter was back. She kept hearing the words "I need you, Mom" over and over in her head. But she was determined not to give in. She would not compromise her life, not even for her new granddaughter. She'd given enough.

The baby made soft grunting noises. Her hunger now satisfied, she was squirming to get comfortable. Martha took the baby to her own room, and laid her down on the bed, and as she fell asleep a smile formed on her lips. "She's dreaming about angels," Martha's mother used to say about Laura. "That's why babies smile while they sleep; they can still remember the angels they left behind in heaven." It had been such a beautiful and simple explanation.

"But where had the angels gone as my daughter was growing up?" Martha startled herself by speaking out loud.

The baby had not been awakened by her voice. She sat and watched her, and listened to the softness of her breathing. She felt herself lulled by its cadence. "Sleep, little Martha, sleep," she whispered to her tiny granddaughter.

"Mom, I need you." Laura's voice brought her back from her meditative state.

Martha sighed deeply.

"Mom?"

"I'm coming, I'm coming," she said softly, almost to herself.

She walked on tiptoe so as not to waken the baby, but quickly so as to meet her daughter's need.

I. Response Journal

After reading the story, work with the Response Journal Questions. Share your answers in small groups. Each group will select one question and discuss the response with the class.

1. What are your family's life rhythms? How are they similar to or different from the ones of the family in the story?

_____

_____

_____

2. Have you gone through a rebellious period as a teenager? Do you remember how you felt at the time?

_____

_____

_____

3. How is the mother in the story similar to or different from your mother? Do you or does anyone you know have an attitude similar to the daughter's?

_____

_____

_____

_____

4. How would you feel about being a single parent?

_____

_____

_____

_____

_____

_____

_____

5. Are there any questions or comments you would make to the mother or daughter?

_____

_____

_____

_____

_____

_____

_____

II. Mapping the Story

Use the chart that follows to map out the story. Show how the author reveals what the characters are like and the conflicts of each character. While the mother's problems are more clearly stated, you will have to infer the daughter's struggles through clues from the story. In groups of three, compare and discuss the story map. In whole-class discussion, come to a consensus for each item on the chart.

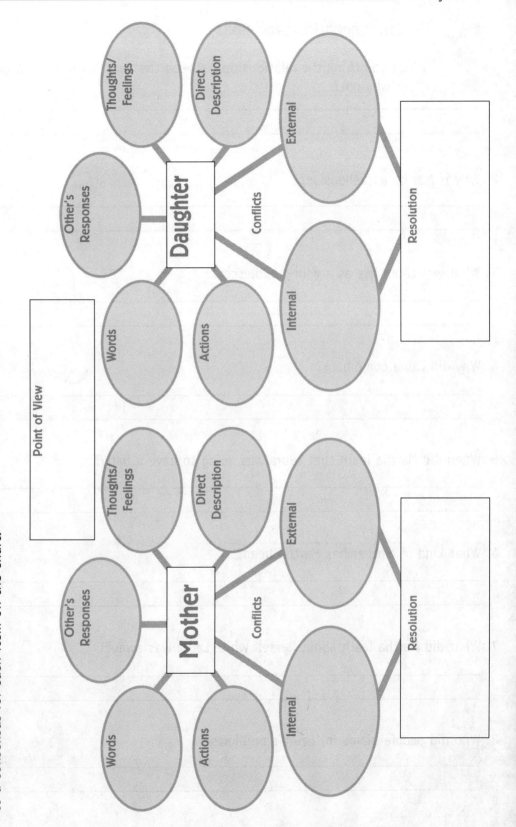

III. Comprehension Questions

1. Do you think the relationship between the two characters is a good one? Why or why not?

_____

_____

2. Why is Martha apprehensive?

_____

_____

3. What was Laura like as a young adolescent?

_____

_____

4. Why did Laura come back?

_____

_____

5. When did Martha learn that Laura was going to have a baby?

_____

_____

6. What kind of mother has Martha been?

_____

_____

7. What did Martha learn about herself while Laura was away?

_____

_____

8. Who did people blame for Laura's problems?

_____

_____

IV. Looking More Closely

Establish the chronology of the events of the story through Laura's life.

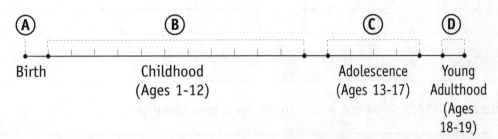

A   B   C   D

Birth   Childhood   Adolescence   Young

(Ages 1-12)   (Ages 13-17)   Adulthood

(Ages 18-19)

Put the events in the period in which they happened by writing the letter of the period in the space provided.

1. Laura leaves her home and says she is independent. _____

2. Laura breaks her thumb-sucking habit. _____

3. Martha learns that Laura is going to have a baby. _____

4. Martha thinks about how Laura's life will be as she grows up. _____

5. Laura and Martha spend time in the offices of several therapists. _____

6. Martha reclaims her life. _____

7. Martha faces many confrontations with school officials. _____

V. Springboard

Expressing Your Views

On your own, answer the following questions. Share your ideas with the class.

1. What do you think would be the ideal relationship between children and their parents after the children become adolescents?

_____

_____

_____

_____

_____

2. What do you think causes children to rebel against their parents?

_____

_____

_____

_____

_____

3. Write about the best advice your parents have ever given you.

_____

_____

_____

_____

_____

4. Why was this good advice?

_____

_____

_____

_____

_____

_____

5. Did you think it was good advice at first, or did you disagree with your parents?

_____

_____

_____

_____

_____

6. When you realized that the advice was helpful, did you thank your parents?

_____

_____

_____

_____

Analyzing the Issues

Work together. Select two questions from the following and follow the directions given for each question.

1. If a young, single woman becomes pregnant, who do you think should have the responsibility of caring for the baby? Why? Should the young woman's parents be expected to support the baby? Why? Why not? Share your ideas in small groups. Be prepared to present them for class discussion.

_____

_____

_____

_____

2. In small groups, discuss the following questions. Write down your ideas and be prepared to share them with the class.

a. Usually in school settings, we do not discuss the needs of parents. Do you think this is a topic that should be given attention in the classroom? Why? Why not? In your discussion decide what you consider to be those needs.

b. Society often blames parents for their children's misdeeds. Do you agree that parents should be held responsible for their children's misconduct? Why? Why not?

3. With a partner try to find information about young single parents. You may wish to consult magazines, journals, newspapers and the Internet. Sometimes psychology textbooks will have information on this issue.

a. How are young single mothers affected?
Do most single mothers complete high school?
Do most of them go to college?
How has having a child early in life affected their lives?

_____

_____

_____

_____

_____

_____

b. How are young fathers being affected?
Are more young men becoming involved with their children?
Do these young fathers get to complete their education?
What kinds of jobs do they find?

_____

_____

_____

_____

_____

_____

c. How are the babies affected?
Are these babies well cared for?
Who usually takes care of them?

_____

_____

_____

_____

_____

_____

d. What special needs and problems will these young parents and their children face?

_____

_____

_____

_____

_____

_____

With your partner, put together an informative pamphlet that presents the pros and cons of young, single parenthood.

2. The Caribbean Pearl

Brainstorming

Make a list of the words that come to your mind after reading the title.

_____   _____   _____

_____   _____   _____

_____   _____   _____

_____   _____   _____

Discuss the list with the rest of the class.

Make Your Prediction

What do you think the story is going to be about?

_____

_____

_____

_____

The Caribbean Pearl

Terry Mezo

The town of Naguabo is located on the eastern coast of the island of Puerto Rico. It is a small town with high hills and very narrow, curvy roads with shady mango, oak and flamboyan trees that flourish on both sides. The trees are so thick that the road is totally shaded, but during the night the road becomes sinister. It is like driving through this dark, pitch-black tunnel. You can't see anything! In fact, it's very scary. However, during the day you can admire the beauty of the coastal ocean while driving along these shores. There are many small *kioskos*, small restaurants that sell fish supplied by fishermen who live in the small fishing village called Hucares.

Saúl, a fisherman from this village, has a nine-year-old son who also wants to be a fisherman. Every morning they wake up at 4:00 a.m. to prepare for their fishing trip. Father and son begin their workday walking down the steep hills, feeling the morning dew refresh their cheeks as they chat happily on their way to their boat. Five minutes after rowing into the ocean, fishing rods and net ready for their first catch, they turn to look at Playa Hucares to enjoy the peace and quiet felt only in the early hours of the day. This tranquil time cannot compare to the later hours of the day when crowds of people stop to buy fresh fish and eat delicious *arepas*, fried dough, for lunch. While Saúl and his son observe the shores, they see the majestic castle that stands on the far end of the pier. Its architectural details make it intriguing, particularly because it is different from the small, humble homes of the villagers. The castle has bright cobalt blue tiles decorating the roofs and it is painted bright pink, with its old-fashioned French windows facing the sea. It has tall cone-shaped towers, like a very old run-down miniature sample of Disney World's castle. Many people say this castle is haunted and the children of the neighborhood do not dare come near the house. Samuel is hypnotized by the mystery this place holds.

"Father, tell me about this castle!" Samuel asks.

Saúl says, "Well, it is said that many years ago the man who built this castle loved the sea and guarded this coast. Thieves have tried to break into the castle but are scared off by the spirit of this man. Some people say that you can see spirits floating around in the living room."

"One day I will go in," Samuel replies.

"Remember, it's private property," Saúl reminds his son. By 7:45 they had caught the usual number of fish they sell in one day.

Saúl tells Samuel to hurry or he will be late to school.

Two weeks later Samuel wakes up earlier than usual. It is only 3:30 a.m. He jumps out of bed, prepares his fishing rod, and he heads towards the castle. He has other ideas in mind. It is very dark outside, but he isn't afraid. As he approaches the castle, he hears some voices and sees some dim lights inside. His curiosity grows stronger so he walks directly towards the house. As he enters the front gate he feels a little nervous, but he goes on. He wanders around the house and stops when he is faced with the ocean.

"What a wonderful sight," he thinks. He stands there in awe of the splendor of the tranquil sea. Suddenly, he notices there are some translucent fish jumping for joy out of the water as if they were playing hide and seek. Samuel leaves the castle, compelled by the parade of brilliantly colored tropical fish he has seen. Orange, blue, yellow, green, red, and even pink are the parading fish. He gets into his father's boat and rows to take a closer peek at these colorful fish when out of the water jump two radiant, orange fish.

"Wow!" Samuel shouts. "You are gorgeous! Why do you shine so bright?"

One of the fish sticks his head out of the water and replies, "I shine this bright because I am the messenger of the sea."

Samuel is baffled, in total shock. "I must be dreaming. I can't be hearing a fish talk," he says to himself.

"Well, you're not crazy. I can talk," replies the orange fish. "I am a clown fish that cannot smile anymore. There is an important message you must pass on to your people and especially the kids. Many fish are getting sick and dying; the waters are contaminated by the amounts of trash dumped in the sea." The fish continues, "I have been to the coast of Fajardo, from where I have seen the beautiful Conquistador and the Seven Seas. I have been to Luquillo's deep oceans near the *kioskos*. I've been to Cabo

Rojo's shores and have seen the exotic lighthouse. I've been to Mar Chiquita. I've been to Aguadilla's Crash Boat Beach, and even to San Juan's coastal seas which placidly touch El Morro's shores. All the fish are suffering from the same problem, too. Please tell your friends and neighbors that we are dying of polluted waters. God blessed this small island. It is the paradise of the Caribbean Sea. Your own people are killing its beauty. We, the fish dwelling in your waters, are worried about your future. Go and tell your friends at school to take care of this chosen Pearl."

In total amazement, Samuel rows to the shore as fast as he can. When he looks towards the castle, he sees floating human shadows waving at him as if saying good-bye or hello. While he hurries back home, he hears voices coming from the castle whispering soft-sounding words carried through the air "Samuel... save our island... save... save our Paradise".

I. Response Journal

After reading the story, work with the Response Journal Questions. Share your answers in small groups. Each group will select one question and discuss the responses with the class.

1. How do you feel after reading the story? Do you think Samuel will do something to help save the Earth?

_____

_____

_____

_____

_____

2. What do you think of the fish's advice? Why do you think a fish, not a person, gives the advice?

_____

_____

_____

3. How do you feel about what people are doing to the Earth?

_____

_____

_____

_____

4. Did you ever have an opportunity as a child to explore a new place that made a big impression on you?

_____

_____

_____

_____

_____

5. Have you or anyone you know had an experience with a haunted house? Tell the group about it.

_____

_____

_____

_____

_____

II. Mapping the Story

Fill in the story map below to show how the elements of literature identified are important for the theme of the story. In groups of three, compare and discuss the story map. In whole-group discussion, come to a consensus for each item on the chart.

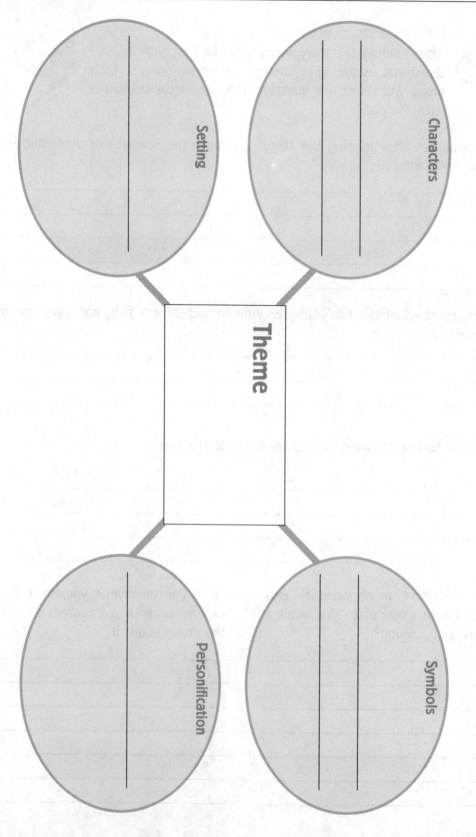

Characters

Setting

Theme

Symbols

Personification

III. Comprehension Questions

1. What makes the roads in Naguabo so unique?

_____

_____

_____

2. How does the man in the story make a living?

_____

_____

_____

3. At what time does the fisherman begin his fishing routine?

_____

_____

_____

4. Who helps him every morning?

_____

_____

_____

5. What is the boy curious about?

_____

_____

_____

6. What did the boy do in the second week of the story?

_____

_____

_____

7. What happened to him?

_____

_____

_____

IV. Looking More Closely

1. Have you ever been fishing? What was it like?

_____

_____

_____

_____

2. Write about the beaches you consider to be the most beautiful.

_____

_____

_____

_____

3. Have you ever driven through dark, curvy roads at night? If so, did it frighten you?

_____

_____

_____

_____

4. Do you believe in ghosts? Do you think we can receive messages from the other world?

_____

_____

_____

_____

5. What is the important message the boy is supposed to give his friends? Why?

_____

_____

_____

_____

6. How realistic do you think the story is?

_____

_____

_____

_____

7. Have you ever seen a ghost?

_____

_____

_____

_____

8. What famous stories or tales are you familiar with that tell about ghosts and superstitions?

_____

_____

_____

_____

_____

V. Reflecting Further on the Story
Work with a partner and be prepared to share your answers with the class.

1. What is the problem presented in the story ? What do you think will be some of the consequences if the people do not take the boy's message seriously? Discuss.

_____

_____

_____

_____

2. If you had a similar experience, how do you think you would react?

_____

_____

_____

_____

3. Ask your grandparents or a contemporary of theirs if they remember any of the stories about superstitions or ghosts from their days. Report to the class.

_____

_____

_____

_____

4. What is a ghost? Do you believe they exist? Are ghosts and spirits the same thing? Explain.

_____

_____

_____

_____

5. Write a list of superstitions and discuss them with your class.

_____   _____   _____

_____   _____   _____

_____   _____   _____

_____   _____   _____

6. Is there any part of the world which you think might not be polluted? Explain where and why.

_____

_____

_____

_____

VI. Springboard

Collaborative Activities
Work in groups of three or four. Make a list of the environmental problems affecting the world today.

_____   _____   _____

_____   _____   _____

_____   _____   _____

Discuss your lists of environmental issues with your classmates.

Researching a Topic
Work in groups of three or four. Each group will select one of the environmental problems in the previous activity. Search for information on the problem your group selects. Read articles in newspapers and magazines or search on the Internet. Present your findings to the rest of the class. In addition, suggest possible solutions for the problem.
What can be done to awaken concern regarding this matter?
What serious consequences will be felt if action is not taken?

Optional Each group can work on a poster board that illustrates group members' ideas about the environmental problem you have researched. You can use your poster board to report to the class. Bring in crayons, glue, scissors, and magazines for the activity.

Expressing Your Views

What can the government do to get people involved in helping with ecological problems?

_____

_____

_____

Do you the think the government should obligate people to recycle?

_____

_____

_____

On Your Own
1. List five causes of pollution and five items that can be recycled.
2. Work with a partner and propose a recycling program. Find out what other countries are doing about recycling and how effective their programs are. Complete the recycling chart below.

Collaborative Activity
Play a guessing game. The teacher will prepare cards with causes of pollution. Using a paper clip or tape, the teacher will place a card on each student's back. The students will walk around and give clues to each other to help guess what cause of pollution they represent.

The same procedure can be used for the following variation of the game: The teacher will write the names of different kinds of pollution or recyclable items on cards. You will write information about what appears on your card and present orally to the rest of the students for them to guess what you are.

3. Panas

1. Look at the list of countries and write the name of a fruit or food that you associate with that particular place. In small groups, compare your lists. Are there some fruits and foods that appear more than others? What are the most popular foods on the lists?

Country	Fruit	Other Food
China		
Italy		
The Dominican Republic		
Mexico		
The United States		
Spain		
Cuba		
Argentina		
Puerto Rico		

2. Write down your answers to the following questions and then share them with your classmates.
a. Have you ever been curious about a fruit that is different or strange to you?

_____

_____

_____

b. Are you familiar with the trees and plants that grow in your country?

_____

_____

_____

c. If you had to be away from your native country for a very long time, what things would you miss? Why?

_____

_____

_____

_____

d. Do you think you would feel the same about them when you returned?

_____

_____

_____

_____

3. Prediction
Based on the above questions, what do you think this story will be about?

_____

_____

_____

_____

Panas

Rosa A. Vallejo

I place the plate of boiled breadfruit pieces in front of my mother and my husband. They have been hungrily waiting for their lunch. Next to the breadfruit plate I place another filled to the brim with cooked salted codfish, sliced tomatoes, onions and avocados. I set down a flask of olive oil, and they eagerly dig in.

My husband had selected and cut the breadfruit from the tree that stands at the back of our backyard. My mother, in her advanced years, is convinced that someone enters our backyard and takes the breadfruit from our tree. She has been carefully watching them from the window in her room and is ready for her reward.

I watch them eat, but I do not partake of the feast. Breadfruit does not hold the same fascination for me as it holds for them. I eat it once in a while, but I can't muster up the excitement that seems to overtake them when the fruit first appears on the tree.

"Why do I love this stuff so much?" my mother asks herself. "I guess it's because I grew up on it."

"No," my husband says, "loving *panas* is the mark of being a true Puerto Rican."

I roll my eyes. I know where this is headed. My husband is making digs at the fact that I did not grow up on the Island. I was raised in New York City, and therefore I'm not considered authentic. My ethnicity is instead defined as *Newyorican*.

"You're right," I say. "There aren't too many breadfruit trees growing in New York."

He's too busy chewing to answer me, and as I watch them eat, my mind wanders off to my very first encounter with the great *pana*.

"*Panas! Panas!*" I can almost hear my sister's voice shouting at me as she points to the strange globes on the table.

"These are *panas!*" She says this with joy and a broad smile.

I watch her and my cousin pick up the green globes and smell and pat them. They seem to be in some sort of trance as they inhale whatever fragrance is coming from the strange round fruit. I wasn't sure how I was expected to react. Vegetables and fruits are not the kinds of things that evoke great feelings in me one way or another. We were visiting my cousin in the countryside of Luquillo. It was my first trip to Puerto Rico, and my sister was trying to impress me with all the small wonders of the island.

We had just arrived at the small wooden structure which was my cousin's temporary house, and my sister, upon being told that *panas* were being cooked for lunch, had made a mad dash for the tiny kitchen at the back of the house. I was more impressed by my cousin's house. It looked like a wooden dollhouse. I was shocked at the size of it and appalled that she would have left her nice apartment in the Bronx for this.

"Come," her husband said to me. "I want to show you something."

We walked outside and he pointed to a construction site a few feet away. Concrete blocks already formed the foundation of what was to be their permanent home.

"I work on it during the afternoons and weekends, so it's going a little slow," he said.

"You're building the house all by yourself?" I could picture my cousin living in that little wooden dollhouse for the next twenty years. He started to say something, but at that moment my sister came running out of the house, grabbed my hand and pulled me along until we stood under a tree.

"This," she said, "is a *pana* tree."

It seemed to me that she was making some sort of formal introduction. Again, I wasn't quite sure how to react.

"It's very nice," I said and proceeded to move away.

"It's wonderful," she whispered, and yanked me back.

"Yeah, yeah, it's a pretty nice tree." I felt that I had paid enough homage.

"You don't understand," she said. "It's a *pana* tree."

"You said that already. What's the big…" I stopped in mid-sentence because when I looked at her she had tears in her eyes. She was right. I did not understand.

"We had two beautiful trees like this one on our land." All of a sudden she sounded sad. "Often, *panas* were all we had to eat." She looked at me and forced a smile. "You know, I didn't think they were so great then. Sometimes I even hated them. They seemed symbolic of our poverty. Now, I can't wait to eat those *panas* and I think this is one of the most beautiful trees to grow on this island. Our trees were not very important to me. I took them for granted the way I did everything that was a part of my life then. I didn't realize then that everything that surrounded me—all the trees, the plants, and the flowers—were actually an extension of myself. I was — part of this island too. Now, I miss that life."

I looked at the tree. Its large frond-like leaves were waving gently in the breeze. There were round, green globes hanging here and there from its branches. It was a fine-looking tree, but I could not connect with it the way I did with the beautiful oaks and elms that I encountered in the New York City parks.

"How about a nice cup of coffee to round out this great lunch?" My husband startles me back to reality and my own kitchen.

While they sip their coffee, I decide to walk down to the breadfruit tree. The mid-afternoon sun, hot and bright, makes the leaves shimmer in the slight wind that stirs up every so often. I never walk down to this tree so I make my way carefully around the banana plants and palm trees that are my husband's pride and joy. Since the land has a downward slope, I am afraid that my first encounter with the tree will be headfirst.

I stop several feet away from the tree so that I can observe it from a distance. I can remember when my husband first planted it. The tree was a gift from my cousin, an offshoot from the first breadfruit tree I had been introduced to by my sister. That tree still stands and now shades the terrace of my cousin's lovely five-bedroom house, but this tree has surpassed its parent tree in height and its leafy head has spread out several feet to the sides. There are still several green full-sized breadfruits hanging from its branches, and as I stand under it looking up through its wide leaves I remember my sister's insistence that I somehow could not understand the difference between a *pana* tree and the trees I had grown up with. I close my eyes and think back to my mother's words: "I grew up on this stuff." I imagine that I see my grandmother standing under a similar tree, trying to decide which of the round *panas* she will select for her children's dinner. Perhaps she learned how to pick just the perfect *pana* from her own mother, my great-grandmother, who probably learned it from my great-great-grandmother.

I have to laugh at myself. I've gathered generations of women under that tree. But although I feel rather foolish for being so dramatic, I'm also glad that I've learned what a *pana* is, and that my children look at *pana* trees as part of the landscape of their lives. The trees are extensions of themselves.

I hear the phone ringing at the house. "Your sister's on the phone," my husband shouts. My sister still lives in the States and we talk every week. I'm so winded when I get to the phone that I can hardly speak.

"What's the matter with you?" my sister asks with concern in her voice.

"I was down by the *pana* tree." I almost gasp out the words.

"Are there *panas*? Will you be bringing us some when you come? I can't wait!"

I am under no delusions. I know it is the *panas* that she can't wait for. It's those generations of women speaking through her.

✳

I. Response Journal

After reading the story, work with the Response Journal Questions. Share your answers in small groups. Each group will select one question and discuss the response with the class.

1. When you saw the picture of the *pana* at the beginning of the story, what images came to your mind?

_____

_____

_____

_____

2. Have you ever had an experience similar to that of the main character with the *pana* tree?

_____

_____

_____

_____

3. Can you think of anything you may have taken for granted as a child that now is very important to you?

_____

_____

_____

_____

4. What is your identity based on? How closely is it related to your country, community or any other place you have lived?

_____

_____

_____

_____

_____

_____

5. How important do you think it is for a person to have strong roots in terms of nationality and religion?

_____

_____

_____

_____

_____

_____

II. Mapping the Story

Use the chart that follows to map out the story. Show how the different settings and descriptions move the plot along. In groups of three, compare and discuss the story map. In whole-class discussion, come to a consensus for each item on the chart.

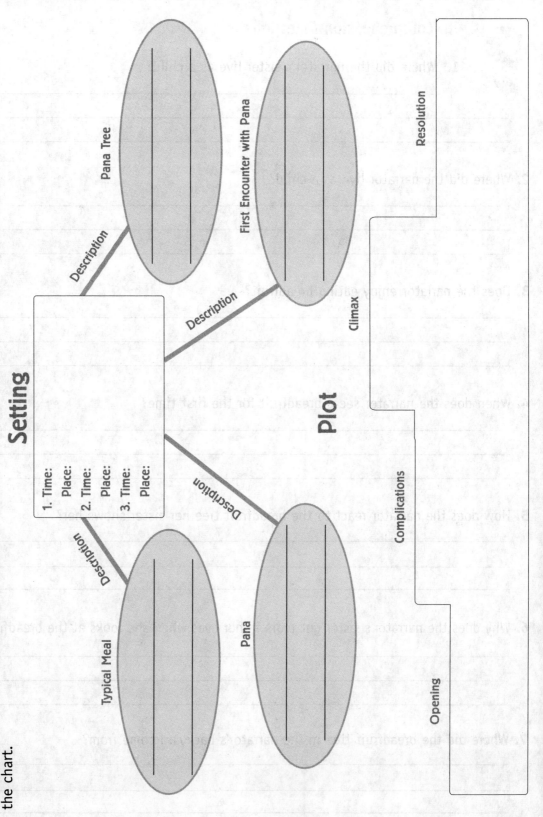

Setting

1. Time:
   Place:
2. Time:
   Place:
3. Time:
   Place:

Description — Pana Tree

Description — First Encounter with Pana

Description — Typical Meal

Description — Pana

Plot

Opening

Complications

Climax

Resolution

III. Comprehension Questions

1. Where did the narrator's sister live as a child?

_____

_____

_____

2. Where did the narrator live as a child?

_____

_____

_____

3. Does the narrator enjoy eating breadfruit?

_____

_____

_____

4. When does the narrator see a breadfruit for the first time?

_____

_____

_____

5. How does the narrator react to the breadfruit tree her sister shows her?

_____

_____

_____

6. Why does the narrator's sister get tears in her eyes when she looks at the breadfruit tree?

_____

_____

_____

7. Where did the breadfruit tree in the narrator's backyard come from?

_____

_____

_____

8. When the narrator goes down to the tree in her backyard, what does it make her think about? Why?

_____

_____

_____

9. Does the cousin's husband finish the house he is building?

_____

_____

_____

10. Where will the narrator be traveling to?

_____

_____

_____

IV. Looking More Closely

A symbol is something that extends meaning in a story. It stands for something else or has a larger meaning. Think of the *pana* in this story. Do you think that it might stand for something more than a fruit? What else might it stand for in the story?

_____

_____

_____

_____

_____

_____

_____

V. Springboard

Expressing Your Views
On your own, answer the following questions. Share your answers with the class.

The narrator of the story states that she is happy that her children have grown up around breadfruit trees. Is there anything about your culture, or a particular tradition that your parents have been especially careful about teaching you? Are you glad they have made this effort? Why? Why not?

_____

_____

_____

_____

_____

_____

_____

Bringing the Story to Your World

With a partner or in a small group, talk about the traditional foods in your culture that you really enjoy. Do you feel differently about eating these foods than you feel about dishes that are more international? Why? Why not? Write down your ideas and share them with the class.

_____

_____

_____

_____

_____

_____

_____

_____

_____

If you had the opportunity to interview someone from a different culture, what would you want to know? Make a list of the questions you would ask. What would you enjoy sharing about your culture? Share your ideas with a partner. Did you come up with many of the same things?

_____

_____

_____

_____

_____

_____

_____

_____

_____

Analyzing the Issues

Work together. Select two of the following questions and follow the directions given for each question.

1. How would you define cultural identity? Write your ideas down and then share them in a small group. Are the other ideas in the group very different from yours or are they similar? Select the ideas that are most repeated and share them with the rest of the class.

_____

_____

_____

_____

_____

_____

_____

_____

_____

_____

_____

2. With a partner, discuss the following question. Present your ideas to the class.

Often the children of people who have migrated to other countries begin to lose some of the traditions and values of their parents' native culture. Do you think that parents should insist that their children maintain these traditions? Why? Why not?

_____

_____

_____

_____

_____

_____

_____

_____

3. In groups of three or four, discuss the following questions. After discussing all the questions, select one and write down the ideas of the group. Present your ideas to the rest of the class for discussion.

Throughout history people have left their native countries and migrated to other countries in search of a better life.

•How do immigrants enrich the dominant culture of a country?
•If these people were to return to their native countries, do you think that they might have a difficult time re-adapting? Why? Why not?
•Do you think it would be more difficult for the children of these people to return to their parents' native country? Why? Why not?

•Do you think that people who return to their native countries have an impact on the culture of that country? Why? Why not?

_____

_____

_____

4. Often our first introduction to a different culture is through food. Many people like to visit ethnic restaurants to try foods that are different from their own. In groups of three or four, discuss the different ethnic restaurants in your city or town.
   Are there many?
   Which ones have you visited?
You may need to check a telephone directory to discover what ethnic restaurants are available to you.
When you visit an ethnic restaurant, what aspects of the culture are you exposed to besides the food?

_____

_____

_____

_____

_____

_____

5. Look at the picture of the breadfruit at the beginning of the story. What is your impression of it? How do you think it might feel to the touch? How do you think it will taste? Would you be interested in tasting it?

_____

_____

_____

_____

_____

4. The Virtual World

You will work in groups of three. Your group will select three different areas to work with from the list below.

You are going to create a NEW WORLD. In this world you will establish new systems and rules. Explain how these will function in the areas you have chosen.
Consider the following questions to help guide you in creating your new world.

- What things would you prohibit? Why?
- What laws would you establish?

Group members:

Areas selected:

Areas:

clothing	music	food	economy
animals	money	banking	media
education	religion	news	environment
transportation	world resources	politics/laws	marketing
housing	communication	stores	
supermarkets	recycling	plants	

2. What are the essential elements you need to make your world a better one?

_____

_____

_____

_____

_____

Task # 2

You must select a president or governor for your world.

Work together with a partner to brainstorm qualities and skills a president or governor should have. List all the characteristics you consider important on the chart below. After completing it, discuss your list with the class.

You will write a definition of what it takes to be a good president or governor using your findings and the questions below to help guide you. Each pair will present their definition to the class orally.

What qualities should the president or governor of your world have?

What academic preparation?

What skills will you require this person to have?

What personal traits, abilities, and attitudes should this person have?

Is it easy to find people with such specifications? Explain why or why not.

Qualities	Skills
_____	_____
_____	_____
_____	_____
_____	_____
_____	_____
_____	_____
_____	_____
_____	_____
_____	_____
_____	_____
_____	_____
_____	_____
_____	_____
_____	_____
_____	_____
_____	_____
_____	_____

The Virtual World

Terry Mezo

It is April 25, 2060. I look out the window of this sixth floor building and all I can see is a black, brown, gray, dull cloud! The rainbow of colors (when visible) comes from the many cars parked on the sidewalks all jammed against each other. Green is not a color included in this rainbow. There are no trees in sight, only large buildings, large masses of cement and heavy damp air that irritates the eyes if you don't wear special glasses. It's extremely hot. I can't remember the last time it rained. The road is continuously steaming fumes that rise high into the air and evolve into dark clouds.

This office where I work helps some women fulfill the most crucial of their desires: the need to be a mother. I just make sure everything runs smoothly. All our customers must be satisfied, and most importantly, all documents have to be completed accurately. Malpractice lawsuits have proliferated so dramatically that any misunderstanding in completing the forms can result in legal prosecution –even jail.

Two women walk through the door and as I greet them I hand them the requisition form they must fill out. They sit near each other and happily chat about the type of child they want to have.

"I'd like my son to be special," one says to the other. "I want him to have deep blue eyes, caramel-colored hair, thin lips, reasonably sized ears, Chinese-shaped eyes and an

Irish nose. I want him to have excellent math skills and a very high IQ. I want him to be an art lover and have exquisite taste in music. In addition, I'd like him to have Brad Pitt's sex appeal, Christopher Reeve's height and humble soul, Antonio Banderas' tan, Robin Williams' sense of humor, Michael Jordan's speed, and Al Pacino's stamina."

"Wow! You sure have given a lot of thought to this," replies the other woman, and they both break out in laughter.

As I listen to the conversation I think about the incredible advances science and technology have brought to the world, but I also think about the effects of these on our world! I never thought about the possibility of actually ordering a baby as if it came from a catalog, and the many limitless possibilities.

Scientists have invented a cloning system, where a person can reorder someone they have lost, or someone they loved. All that is needed is a DNA sample of the person and he or she will be born again. The only thing science has not been able to come up with is the instant growth mechanism for this being to continue on where he or she left off. Many people have reunited with their lost children.

As I look at the computerized screen in our lobby which runs the headlines every half hour, today's astonishing news reads: Hitler's clone has turned ten years old today and Saddam Hussein's nephew is ruling the Middle East. Suddenly, I find myself shivering with an acute stomachache that stops me in the hall. Reflecting on past events in history, and hoping to God that events like the holocaust and biological warfare are events of the past. Here we have Hitler reincarnated again. I can see the other side of scientific advances immediately. I think we have cause for panic! Particularly when the new generations don't seem to be afraid of dying or killing or shooting anyone. They seem to find nothing amusing unless it is violent. In fact, their emotional systems appear to require a daily dose of violence in order to function better. This is reflected in the media and games that they engage in and it's what keeps them entertained. I don't understand how I've lived to see this!

Fortunately, my job deals with the more positive side of science.

I assist the doctor while he interviews a patient. Simultaneously, a data entry clerk feeds the information that appears on her requisition form into the computer and the computer automatically comes up with the picture of the baby she will mother. Now she must decide whether or not she wants to be the gestational mother. There are these incredible incubators which complete the process for her, if she so desires. Many women still want to be the carriers because they understand that bonding is a necessary experience. In the waiting room some women talk about the advantages of being the gestational carrier. One of the women there comments she would like to provide her child with a real family, instead of being a single mother. But because she is over forty she decides to try the system we offer immediately. It catches my attention and gives me joy to see there are still some women that share this idea. Nonchalantly, I walk up to her and invite her to a cup of coffee.

While at the cubicle, the woman drinking coffee asks my opinion about her desire to marry, once she has ordered her child. My reply would have been too old-fashioned for her; therefore I remain silent. Suddenly, the woman says, "I know women don't need a man to conceive a baby and even less to burden themselves with more duties as a wife, especially today when only 2 % of the population believe in marriage. But I still would like to get married and have my own family."

My mind wanders off... I start thinking about how women have gained power in the work force, in the economy and in government and yet families are dysfunctional and unattended. Nevertheless, we women have demonstrated we are competent.

"Well," she says, snapping me back to reality, "do you think I'm foolish for thinking like this?"

"Go ahead with your plans," I reply. "I'm happy for you."

It's been a long day. I'm finally going home. As I stand in front of my door, I realize I can't figure out my entrance code. Everything is so automated, pushing codes and numbers into machines. Our lives seem to be remote, controlled. I feel so old. I see all these advances as gigantic complications. Imagine, I can't even turn on my own TV. I need help when I'm operating these screened phones.

Such sophistication! And I struggle every day just to figure out how to cook the synthetic meals free from radiation, how to set my computerized news in the morning and–worst of all–how to charge my solar operated car battery. This is my daily trauma!

I just want to go back... back to what was normal for me. People used to fall in love, get married, raise their kids, share and talk. There were family values, morals and ethics. There was a sense of belonging. Mothers would breast-feed their infants and spend time with them. Children would socialize and play in schools. Science and technology could not substitute the human role then. Expectant mothers waited for their surprise. Being a single mother was then a sad reality. People wanted to formalize relationships and make commitments!

I am here in this better and extremely advanced world where women decide if they want to be mothers at fifty, at sixty, and whether or not they want to be the gestational carriers too. I'm out of place. I don't belong. At my age, I would be at a nursing home or unemployed if it weren't for my grandson. He is the doctor that runs this office. He understands my need to belong, to be productive, to move on, and be creative. I'm here not allowing machines to take away my skills. I am his receptionist in this scientifically developed office. He has protected me from the segregation of the elderly.

Every now and then, he scolds me for talking too much or for mentally drifting away while looking through this sixth floor window. I'm always hoping to see something green... I'd do anything to see a tree!

✳✳✳

I. Response Journal

After reading the story, work with the Response Journal Questions. Share your answers in small groups. Each group will select one question and discuss the responses with the class.

1. How comfortable would you feel living in the world described in the story?

_____

_____

_____

2. How would you feel about ordering a baby from a catalog?

_____

_____

_____

3. Would you like to be cloned? Why or why not?

_____

_____

_____

_____

4. What kind of person do you think the narrator's grandson is? Would you like to socialize with him?

_____

_____

_____

_____

_____

5. How probable do you think it is for the world to be like the one in the story in the year 2060?

_____

_____

_____

_____

_____

II. Mapping the Story

Use the chart below to map out the story. Show how the setting and imagery (related to the senses) are important to create the atmosphere for the story. Think about how the other elements on the chart also contribute to the atmosphere. In groups of three, compare and discuss the story map. In whole-class discussion, come to a consensus for each item on the chart.

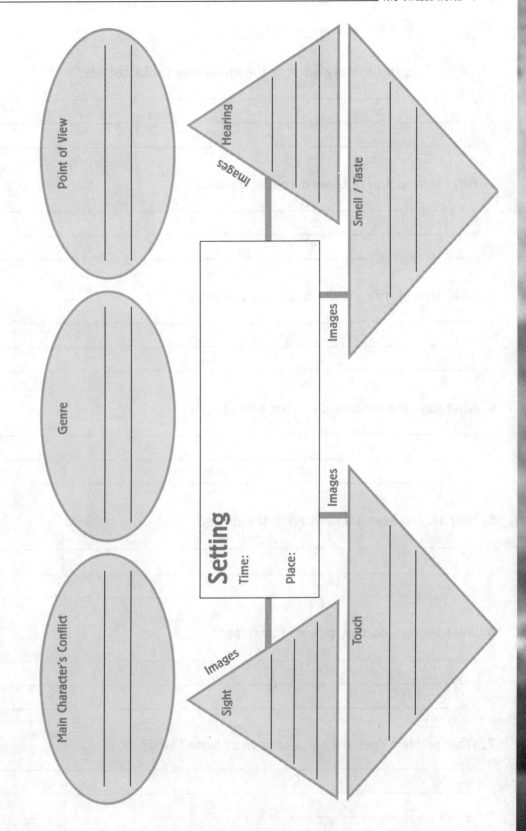

III. Comprehension Questions

1. In the story, what is the environment like outside?

_____

_____

_____

2. Why do people have to wear special glasses?

_____

_____

_____

3. What kind of office is the setting of the story?

_____

_____

_____

4. What does the narrator do in the office?

_____

_____

_____

5. How are the news transmitted in the office?

_____

_____

_____

6. What services do they provide for women?

_____

_____

_____

7. What problem does the narrator have at home? Why?

_____

_____

_____

IV. Looking More Closely

1. Is the narrator a man or a woman? How do you know?

_____

_____

_____

2. What are the narrator's feelings? How are they presented?

_____

_____

_____

3. Do the problems in the story have a solution?

_____

_____

_____

_____

4. Do you see any evidence of stereotypes in the story? If any, what are they?

_____

_____

_____

5. Are there parts of the story that you find humorous? Why?

_____

_____

_____

_____

6. How far do you think science will be able to get in the future?

_____

_____

_____

_____

V. Reflecting Further on the Story

With a partner, choose two items from below to work with and discuss your answers with the class.

1. There are some problems stated in the story and others are implied. Mention four of these problems and the clues that lead you to them:

a. Problem: _____ Clue: _____

b. Problem: _____ Clue: _____

c. Problem: _____ Clue: _____

d. Problem: _____ Clue: _____

2. Is this story realistic or non-realistic? Express your personal view.

_____

_____

_____

3. Which part did you like most? Why?

_____

_____

_____

4. Which part did you like least? Why?

_____

_____

_____

5. Would the world be better if only men or only women ruled? Explain.

_____

_____

_____

6. How are the elderly perceived in this story?

_____

_____

7. Do you think there should be mandatory retirement for people at 65? Explain why or why not.

_____

_____

_____

8. Do you see families today changing in their attitude toward the elderly? How?

_____

_____

_____

VI. Springboard

Collaborative Activity
With a partner, choose two of the areas presented below and predict what you think things will be like in the year 2080.

For example: Careers– Will there be new jobs created in the next millennium? Do you think that jobs that currently exist will disappear? Which ones and why?

Areas:

Money	Banks	Electricity	Transportation
Homes	Environment	Water	Communication
Schools	Media	Food	Careers

Going Beyond
Advances in Technology– Look for a newspaper or magazine article that illustrates some of the advances occurring in the world today. You will summarize the article, find the main idea(s) and present them to the class.

The Importance of Role Models
Choose one of the following activities. Look at the list below. What do you know about the people who are mentioned? Discuss their traits, attributes, and characteristics. Talk about them in class.

1. If you were to order a baby from a catalog, what physical and emotional characteristics would you like this child to have? Why? Whom would you choose as a model? Why?

From the list that follows, choose two role models you know about. If you are not familiar with any of the people on the list, choose two other people you admire. Explain why you selected them.

Mother Teresa of Calcutta	Lady Diana	Dyanara	Martin Luther King
J. F. Kennedy	Ghandi	Rosa Parks	Paulo Paiakan
Michael Jackson	Brad Pitt	Cantinflas	Roberto Clemente
Pope John Paul			

Researching the Topic and Presenting Your Views

Find an article related to the issue of cloning. You can use magazines, newspapers, professional journals, or the Internet.

Summarize the article orally in class. Explain if cloning is visualized positively or negatively in the article. Express your personal view on this matter. If cloning were to become popular, how do you think it would affect our lives?

Take a Stand (Group Work)

You are going to compare the roles of men and women in the future described in the story with those of the past and the present. Are these changes positive, negative or too radical?

* Use the diagram below to work on the activity.

CHANGES

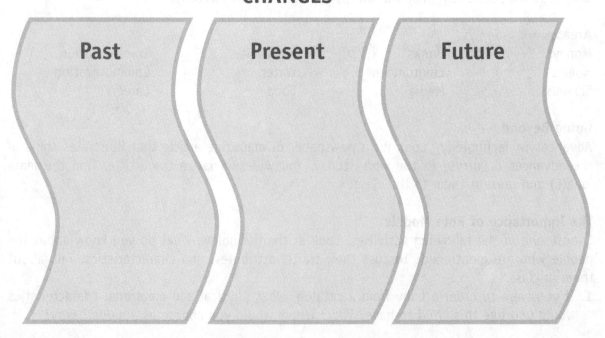

Past   Present   Future

5. Mo-der

On your own, Answer the following questions. Share and compare your answers with a partner.

1. Why do you think children have a need for special people in their lives? _____

_____

2. Other than your mother and father, who did you consider special in your life when you were growing up? _____

_____

3. Do you have a best friend? What characteristics does this person have that your other friends do not have? _____

_____

4. When you get together with your best friend, what kind of activities do you enjoy doing together? _____

_____

5. Have you ever had someone you loved move far away? How did you feel? Did you ever see that person again? _____

_____

Make Your Prediction
Based on the above questions, select the statement that you feel best describes what this story will be about.
a. The story will be about the loss of a best friend.
b. The focus of this story will be on how we can have fun with the people who are special to us.
c. The main idea of this story will be about the importance of special relation-ships in our lives.

Mo~der

Rosa A. Vallejo

A ngie came flying down the stairs from the fifth floor as I was running up to the fourth floor. We collided just as I reached the fourth-floor landing.

"Come on up," she said, "my grandmother has arrived. Come and meet Mother."

She pronounced "mother" as *mo-der*.

"Why are you talking with an accent?" I asked. "You know how to speak English. And why do you have your hair in braids?"

Her usually wiry black hair was bound up in two tight braids.

"Man, are you stupid. That's the way we call her. Everyone calls her *mo-der*, not mother. And," she put a heavy emphasis on the word "mo-der says braids will make my hair straight."

Both ideas sounded really dumb to me, but I didn't want Angie on my bad side, so I didn't say so. Besides she had told me her grandmother made the best *tostones*[1] in the world, and I didn't want to chance missing out on those. Angie had been bragging about her grandmother's visit for weeks.

"Why do you call her *mo-der* instead of *abuelita*[2] or *abuela*[3] or *mamá*[4]?"

---

[1] Fried plantain chips
[2] Diminutive of *abuela*
[3] Grandmother
[4] A word for "mother" that is often used for grandmothers.

She rolled her eyes. "Because, stupid, *mo–der* sounds more like an important title. It sounds something like big *mamí*.[5] Everyone wants to let mother know how important and special she is. The only thing is, we pronounce it in Spanish, *mo–der*. Do you see now?"

I really did not see, but I didn't argue about that either. I didn't like to get Angie angry. She was two years older than me, and really thought that made her a lot smarter. So I wasn't going to risk sounding stupid again. Besides Angie was a special friend. Her family was the only other Puerto Rican family in our building. And, even though she was older and went to a private religious school while I went to a public school, we liked to spend time together whenever we could. I had other friends from school, but Angie was different. She understood some things my other friends did not. I didn't always have to be explaining everything to her. I didn't have to explain that eating boiled green bananas was not going to make you sick, or that the reason I wasn't allowed to ride a bike was because that was something only *machitos* [6] do. Actually, I thought that was a pretty stupid reason not to let me ride a bike, but that was the rule at home. Bikes were for boys. Angie understood because her parents had some weird ideas, too. Some things you just had to be Puerto Rican to understand.

I couldn't visit Angie every day because another rule at home was that I shouldn't be in *casa ajena*[7] all the time. Girls were supposed to be in their own house most of the time. But I loved to go to Angie's apartment because her windows faced out to the street. Our favorite game was to sit by the window to watch the cute boys go by and make fun of all the other girls from the block. When Angie came to visit me, we would look out the window too, but since my apartment faced the back alley the only interesting things to look at were the clothes hung out to dry on lines that crisscrossed one another across the alleyway like a giant cat's cradle. Angie didn't come down too often but when she did, we had fun trying to figure out who had the largest underwear hanging out to dry.

Angie was good at sharing, too. Since she always had more money than I did, she would buy me my favorite treat: salted pumpkin seeds. She let me know she thought it was quite stupid to choose pumpkin seeds as your favorite treat, but she bought them for me anyway. Like I said, she was a special friend.

The door to her apartment was open, so we ran in, and Angie started calling her grandmother at the top of her lungs. "Mo–der, Mo–der!'" It almost sounded like she was saying "murder, murder!"

"*Ay Angelina María, por favor*!" [8] Angie's mother yelled. "Stop running or the lady downstairs will start complaining to the super about the noise again. Please act like young ladies."

Angie slowed down and glanced at me. We both knew that when her mother called

---

[5] Mommy
[6] Diminutive of "macho" or little men
[7] Someone else's house
[8] "Oh, Angelina Maria, please"

her by her full name she meant business. So we both acted the way we thought young ladies would act. We put our hands on our hips and sauntered into Angie's bedroom.

Mo-der was sitting on the bed looking at some of Angie's school pictures. She had on a flowered housedress with a tie around her waist. The tie, which was of the same material as the dress, had been made into a bow and sat right over her left hip. She was the color of cinnamon, and her gray hair was tied into a bun. She looked very small and fragile to me. She smiled when we walked in and pulled Angie to her.

"*Mi Angelina, mi angelito*," [9] she said softly to Angie. "These are such pretty pictures of you."

I stood there feeling a little jealous of the attention Angie was getting. But then Mo-der pulled me to her, too. She hugged and kissed me like she had always known me. She acted as if I were her granddaughter, too. She smelled wonderful, just like the Spanish soap my mother kept in her drawer to make her fancy nightgowns smell good. When she finally stopped hugging and kissing us, Angie introduced me.

Mo-der touched my face and said "*Dios te bendiga, hijita*." [10] What beautiful long hair you have. I bet if I braid it you will have some waves in it tomorrow. You know braids make kinky hair straight but they also make straight hair wavy."

I had always wanted curly hair. This was like a dream come true. "Will you braid my hair, please?" I could already see the looks of envy from my classmates when they saw my hair in waves.

"Sure, sure, of course I will. But first come and eat. I made something special for you girls. I made some *sopa de arroz con leche*. Come, come."

I really hated *sopa de arroz con leche*. In my house they only made this milk and rice soup when someone was sick, but that day I ate every bit that Mo-der served me. I didn't want to disappoint her.

Later Angie and I sat on the stairs next to my apartment. We were both in braids.

"You know, Mo-der reminds me of my grandmother, Mamá Filó, in Puerto Rico."

Angie looked at me with her 'Man, are you stupid' look again.

"You don't even know what your grandmother Filó looks like. You were almost a baby the last time you saw her."

"But my sister Mercedes describes her to me all the time, and she remembers. She was almost fifteen when we came to live in New York. My sister says that Mamá Filó would always hug us and kiss us and say, 'Dios te bendiga.' And she told me that Mamá Filó made *arroz con leche* soup whenever we went to visit." The *arroz con leche* part wasn't really true, but I thought it would help my argument.

Angie just looked at me. This time her look didn't accuse me of being stupid. She was very quiet.

---

[9] "My Angelina, my little angel."
[10] "God bless you, little daughter."

All of a sudden I was very angry at her. "And I bet Mamá Filó smells like Spanish soap, too!" I was almost shouting. "You're not the only one with a grandmother from Puerto Rico, you know."

To my surprise, Angie looked at me and put her arm around me and gave me a big hug. "You know," she said, "I think you are probably remembering your grandmother just the way she is. I'm sure she smells just like Spanish soap, and I bet she makes great *tostones* too."

"Oh yes, that too! That's just the way my grandmother is–just like yours!"

Like I said, Angie was a special friend. She always understood.

I. Response Journal

After reading the story, work with the Response Journal Questions. Share your answers in small groups. Each group will select one question and discuss the response with the class.

1. Why do you think Angie acted the way she did at the end of the story? How did you feel about the ending?

_____

_____

_____

2. Have you ever been jealous of a relationship you have seen between two other people?

_____

_____

_____

3. What makes the grandmother so special?

_____

_____

_____

_____

_____

4. In what ways is the grandmother like your own or someone else's grandmother you have known?

_____

_____

_____

_____

_____

_____

5. How important do you think it is for people to be from the same background to become close friends?

_____

_____

_____

_____

_____

_____

II. Mapping the Story

Use the chart below to map out the story. Show how the different literary elements influence the theme. In groups of three, compare and discuss the story map. In whole-class discussion, come to a consensus for each item on the chart.

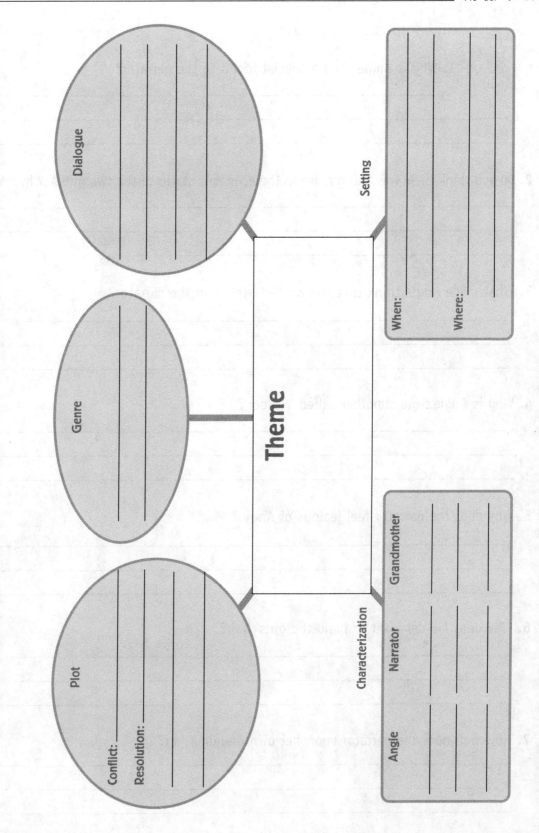

Dialogue

Setting

When:

Where:

Genre

Theme

Plot

Conflict:

Resolution:

Characterization

Angie   Narrator   Grandmother

III. Comprehension Questions

1. Why is Angie such a special friend to the narrator?

_____

_____

_____

2. Do you think there was a difference in the economic status of the two girls? Why? Why not?

_____

_____

_____

3. What made Angie think that she was smarter than the narrator?

_____

_____

_____

4. Why is Angie's grandmother called 'Mo-der'?

_____

_____

_____

5. Why does the narrator feel jealous of Angie?

_____

_____

_____

6. Why does Mo-der want to braid the girls' hair?

_____

_____

_____

7. How well does the narrator know her own grandmother?

_____

_____

_____

8. Do you think that the narrator's parents would have allowed her to play on a baseball team? Why? Why not?

_____

_____

_____

9. Why does the narrator say that her grandmother smells like Spanish soap and that she makes _sopa de arroz con leche_?

_____

_____

_____

IV. Springboard

Expressing Your Views
On your own, answer the following questions. Share your ideas with the class.

1. If you were the narrator, what would you be interested in knowing about your grandmother? What would you tell your grandmother about yourself? Make a list of the things that come to your mind.

_____

_____

_____

Write a letter from the narrator to her grandmother using the information from your list. Share your letters with the class.

_____

_____

_____

_____

_____

_____

_____

_____

_____

_____

2. Think about your best friend. How did s/he become your best friend? Think of the events that led to your special friendship. Are there any similarities in the relationship between you and your best friend and the one between Angie and the narrator?
Is there anything that could cause your friendship to change?

_____

_____

_____

_____

Analyzing the Issues

Work together. Select two of the following questions and follow the directions given for each one.

1. Today, families are often divided by distance. Job opportunities and responsibilities often require people to move from one place to another. Many times children do not get to interact with their extended families. In small groups, discuss ways in which families can maintain a close relationship even when they are far from each other.

a. What special problems do families face when they live far away from their relatives? Think of the children, the elderly, and the working parents in these families. What special needs might they have?

_____

_____

_____

b. How important are friendships to families who live far from other family members?

_____

_____

_____

c. Do you think friends can help fill in the gaps left by relatives who live far away? Be prepared to share your ideas with the class.

_____

_____

_____

_____

2. Although Angie had a good relationship with her grandmother, we often hear that there is a generation gap between the elderly and young people, particularly between the elderly and adolescents. With a partner or in small groups, discuss your feelings on this subject. Do you think there is a generation gap?

Together come up with a list of situations that might cause friction between the elderly and adolescents.

For each item on your list come up with a way to resolve or ease the friction.

Situation	Resolution
_____	_____
_____	_____
_____	_____
_____	_____
_____	_____
_____	_____
_____	_____
_____	_____
_____	_____
_____	_____

3. Think ahead to the future. How do you think you will look when you are 75 years old? Try to draw a picture of yourself at that age or write a description of how you imagine you will look. How do you visualize your life then? Where do you hope to be living? What do you think you will be doing? How would you like to be treated by the younger people? In small groups, share your ideas. Are there any similarities in how the members of the group view the future? Present your ideas to the class for discussion.

6. An Angel in My Path

Collaborating

1. With a partner, discuss the following questions. Together decide on an answer for each question. Share your answers with the class.

a. Do you believe in angels? Write your own definition of an angel. Share your definition with the class. How is your definition different from those of your classmates?

_____

_____

_____

b. What are the characteristics that are usually used to describe angels?

_____

_____

c. Why do you think the topic of angels has become so popular?

_____

_____

d. Where do you think angels live, in heaven or within you?

_____

_____

e. Are you capable of doing good to or for people around you?

_____

_____

f. Are you the type of person who helps others or who prefers to be helped?

_____

_____

On Your Own

1. Take a few minutes and think about the people you saw doing good deeds this week. What was the last "good Samaritan" act that you witnessed? Narrate this experience orally or in writing for the rest of the class.

_____

_____

_____

_____

2. Write your answer to the following question. When you see someone with a flat tire on the street, do you stop to help? Why? Why not? In whole-class discussion, share your answer with the rest of the class.

_____

_____

_____

_____

An Angel in My Path

Rosa A. Vallejo

"Mom, I'll be home on time," my youngest daughter informed me. "Guess what! I met my guardian angel today. I really mean it. I met a real angel today."

She was calling long distance from Kennedy Airport about to board a flight she had almost missed, and didn't have time for further explanations.

My curiosity was piqued, but there was nothing I could do. I would have to wait for her to arrive so I could get the whole story. But angels invaded my thoughts for the rest of the day. I wondered what kind of angel my daughter had met. Had she really met one of these celestial beings or had she joined the ranks of those who are consumed by what I call "angel mania"? These are people who are espousing and promoting anything angelic, and they are doing a good job, too. Angels seem to be everywhere you look. There are angels staring at you in the most unlikely places. They look at you from calendars, picture frames, wrapping paper and even towels. They appear in all varieties of colors and designs. There are fat cherubic angels; stylized, modern angels; angels that are dressed in multicolor robes; angels dressed in white. Many have halos; others do not. They also come in a multitude of textures and materials. There are ceramic angels, wax angels, wooden angels and angels in all kinds of metals. Angels of gold, silver and bronze abound in all sizes. There are even workshops to help you learn how to get in touch with your real guardian angel.

In fact, many people claim to have been in touch already. Many claim to have been rescued or kept from harm by their guardian angels. Others claim to have been taken by their angels to paradise and back and, not surprisingly, claim to have had extraordinary trips. These miraculous occurrences provide the stuff that best-sellers are made of, and these fill whole sections of shelves in the best of bookstores.

Angels seem to abound over and around us. I personally can remember calling on my guardian angel when I was a child. The catechism nuns encouraged us to do so, and so I did whenever I was jaywalking across a particularly busy street. I'd even ask my angels to watch over my shoulder and guide my pen or pencil when I had to take a test, especially when it was a math test. But I must admit that as I grew older I neglected my angel until I had pretty much put him/her out of my life. And now my daughter was telling me that she had encountered one.

By the time my daughter arrived, my angelic thoughts had produced a state of anxiety in me so she quickly told me her story. It seems that due to some last-minute flight changes in the hectic Christmas travel season, her flight from Washington had been detoured to La Guardia Airport, and she needed to get to Kennedy Airport to make her connecting flight home. For some reason there was no shuttle bus service available that would get her there on time. She decided to take a cab, but discovered she only had a couple of dollars in her wallet. Panic was starting to set in when she sighted an ATM machine. Sighing with relief, she left her bags with a gentleman who had been nice enough to listen to her ranting about her predicaments. He was still standing by her bags when she returned sobbing. The machine was not working. She was sure she would have to miss her flight and spend the night there.

It was then that the miracle took place. The man took out his wallet and pulled out a fifty dollar bill. "If I lend you this money, will you pay me back?" he asked.

"Of course," she said with wide-open eyes.

He handed her the money and she made sure to get his name and address. When she got to the cab, she told the driver the story.

"For sure he was an angel," he said. "Be sure to pay him back. For my part, I'll get you there on time." And he did.

By this time my anxiety was turning to disappointment, and I asked her to describe her angel. "He was a very nice man from Boston," she said.

It seems this particular angel was disguised in the ordinary face, body and clothes of a New Englander. I felt rather cheated. There seemed to be nothing celestial about the man being described. "Why do you think he was a guardian angel?" I asked, feeling somewhat annoyed.

She looked at me incredulously. "Mom, are you for real? It was Kennedy Airport in New York." There was a heavy emphasis when she pronounced New York. "This man handed me, a stranger, fifty dollars. You tell me, Mom, do you think any normal human being would do that?"

I was struck by my daughter's question. It seemed she could not believe that normal, everyday human beings could be capable of such kindness. In her mind they seemed to need a capacity beyond the mere human to be caring individuals.

I was thunderstruck! But I realized that in her young life she had not been given the opportunity to see the good in others beyond her social circle. She had been constantly bombarded with the gruesome media reports of hate and violence. She has been made witness to the horrible deeds human beings are capable of inflicting in the name of patriotism, religion, and ethnicity, as well as for greed and vice. These images are the main attractions not only in news reports but also in books, movies, television programs, and computer games.

"It is no wonder," I thought, "that so many are searching for the goodness of angels." I thought again of the kind gentleman from Boston who had given my daughter a helping hand. Perhaps those with angel mania have not been looking for angels in vain. Perhaps they do indeed surround us. Perhaps we have just been looking for them in the wrong guises. Perhaps we should start looking for the angel in ourselves by acting toward others the way this stranger acted toward my daughter.

It is not the images of angels that we need. It is the actions we ascribe to them that we need to put into practice so that our children will learn that human beings are capable of performing miracles here on earth. And when we are the recipients of those miracles, we should make others witness to them.

Later, my daughter kept her promise to the stranger. We sat down to write a check and a thank you note to a very kind and very human gentleman from New England.

I. Response Journal

After reading the story, work with the Response Journal Questions. Share your answers in small groups. Each group will select one question and discuss the response with the class.

1. What did you imagine the story would be about after reading the title?

_____

_____

_____

2. Have you or has anyone you have known ever had an experience with an angel? If so, tell the group about it. If not, tell the group about an experience with an angel from a book or movie.

_____

_____

_____

3. Have you ever had an experience similar to the one in the story?

_____

_____

_____

_____

_____

4. Explain why you do or do not believe in angels.

_____

_____

_____

_____

_____

5. How did the story leave you feeling?

_____

_____

_____

_____

_____

II. Mapping the Story

Use the chart below to map out the story. Show how the theme of the story is related to characterization (each character's attitude) and plot (conflict and resolution). You will have to infer the information not given directly in the story. In groups of three, compare and discuss the story map. In whole-class discussion, come to a consensus for each item on the chart.

Daughter

Attitude: _____

Conflict: _____

Resolution: _____

Man from New England

Attitude: _____

Conflict: _____

Resolution: _____

Mother

Attitude: _____

Conflict: _____

Resolution: _____

Theme

III. Comprehension Questions

1. What makes the daughter think that the man was probably a guardian angel?

_____

_____

_____

2. Why does the mother believe that many people have "angel mania"?

_____

_____

_____

3. Do you think that the taxi driver may be one of those people with "angel mania"? Why? Why not?

_____

_____

_____

4. What kind of world has the daughter been exposed to by the media?

_____

_____

_____

5. According to the mother, what should people be searching for?

_____

_____

_____

6. To what does the mother ascribe the man's kindness?

_____

_____

_____

7. Do you think the mother wants to believe that the stranger was an angel? Explain your answer.

_____

_____

_____

IV. Looking More Closely

The daughter in the story is stranded in a New York City airport. Do you think this story would have been different if she had been stranded in a small town airport? If your answer is yes, explain why and how it would be different. If your answer is no, explain why.

_____

_____

_____

V. Springboard

Expressing Your Views

On your own, answer questions number 1 and 2. Share your answers with the class.

1. The stranger in the story took a risk by giving the young woman fifty dollars. Would you have taken that risk? Think about the decision you would have made, and why you would have made that particular decision.

_____

_____

_____

2. The young woman and her mother sent the stranger a check for the fifty dollars. Why do you think they felt it was important to pay back the stranger? Would you have paid back the money? Explain your answer.

_____

_____

_____

Question number 3 is optional. Your teacher may want you to present your findings as an oral report.

3. Search for information about angels. You might want to look in an encyclopedia, books, magazines, the Internet, the Bible or other religious writings. Try to discover the different concepts that people have had about angels throughout history. Is your concept of an angel similar to any of the ideas you found? If you were asked to draw a figure of an angel, what would your angel look like? Write a description of your angel. You might want to include a drawing.

If you do not agree with the concept of angels, explain why.

Bringing the Story to Your World
Work with a classmate to answer the following question.

How do you think we should classify the famous people listed below? Were they angels or just good human beings? Think of other people you can add to this list. Share your ideas with the rest of the class.

Mother Teresa of Calcutta   Princess Diana   Martin Luther King

Analyzing the Issues
Work together. Select two questions from the following and follow the directions given for each one.

1. In groups, discuss the impact of the media in people's lives. Do you think that newspapers and news reports focus more on negative stories than positive ones? Explain your answer, and provide examples of stories that have been the focus of news reports in the last week.

   _____

   _____

   _____

   _____

2. In a small group, discuss the following questions. Do you believe that violence on television or movies promotes violence in society? Why? Why not?   Who do you think is responsible for what children watch on television or in the movies? Do you think parents should be the most responsible for this, or are filmmakers and television producers equally responsible? Make a list of the programs presented on television that you think are suitable for children. Share your list with the class.

   _____

   _____

   _____

   _____

   _____

   _____

   _____

3. Browse through today's newspaper and select a story that focuses on something good or positive. Bring it to class and share your article with four classmates. Select one of the articles and share it with the class. How many different articles did the class find?

4. Think about someone you know who you feel should receive recognition for giving of him-self/herself to others. Think of the ways this person has been a positive influence in some-one's life. Discuss your ideas with a partner, and listen to what your partner has to say about the person s/he has chosen. With your partner, discuss the best way for you to bring this person to the attention of others. You can do it through one of the forms listed or come up with your own way. Choose the one you are most comfortable with.

- Newscast
- Newspaper or magazine article
- Television commercial
- A short story
- An essay
- A poem
- A collage

Help each other put together the projects and present them to the class.

5. In small groups, discuss the questions below. Decide on the best answers presented, and share them with the rest of the class. Be prepared to defend your answers.
- Do you believe goodness can be taught? Who do you think should teach goodness?

_____

_____

- Do you think that something like world hunger can be stopped by human beings, or do we need some sort of divine intervention?

_____

_____

- Do you believe that the world will always be divided into the fortunate and the unfor-tunate? Why? Why not?

_____

_____

- What would you consider as "evil" forces in the world today? What would you consider as "good" forces? Which do you think will triumph over the other? Why?

_____

_____

7. Virtuoso

Brainstorming

Work with a partner. Brainstorm and fill in the cluster below with what comes to your mind when you see the word "virtuoso."
Discuss your cluster with the class.

Virtuoso

Make Your Prediction

After completing the cluster, look carefully at the words you have brainstormed and predict what the story is going to be about.

_____

_____

_____

_____

_____

Discuss your predictions with your classmates.

Virtuoso

Terry Mezo

Every day he walked the same route, from 14th Street to 8th Street. He'd make a brief stop near Waverly Place. Then he would walk down to Washington Square Park. He seemed strange, wearing old, dirty and torn hospital clothes as if he had just been released from Bellevue Hospital.

He was very thin, and he had shoulder-length, stringy blond hair, oily and messy, obviously from lack of care. His face was in desperate need of a shave. Who knows when was the last time his hands had held a razor blade. When you looked closely, he did have beautiful light-blue eyes which couldn't be appreciated because of the excessive hair. He walked up and down and around the same area every day during the summer. Ramón, the Puerto Rican deli owner, knew him well and every morning would send one of the guys to deliver him coffee and a bagel for his breakfast. The owner of the Italian pizza parlor located at the corner of Waverly and 8th Street made sure he'd get his calzone and soda for lunch. Sometimes they couldn't find him but knew that sooner or later he'd show up. Many times I saw him searching through trash cans.

This very peculiar man was well-known by the store owners in the neighborhood. He seemed harmless. NYU students greeted him in the morning. How they learned about him remains a mystery to me. He hardly ever spoke a single word. I overheard the deli owner telling someone that he was a Vietnam vet who had left his brain behind.

One day after classes, I was roaming around Washington Square Park and I saw him dragging this old, very old piano. He was holding on to this very thick chain which was somehow attached to some part of the piano. I stood there watching him carefully. Although the piano had small wheels, it was heavy. You could see the effort he made while pulling it because the veins in his neck swelled. The piano, which was old and deteriorated, must have been yellow once. He would walk around the park searching for the perfect spot, where the sun would not shine directly on his face, to place his piano. Passersby, tourists and students stopped to watch him, everyone waiting to see what would happen next. So many questions about this homeless man came to my mind. I wondered where he kept his piano during the winter months and the days when he wasn't dragging it around. I'm sure many of us had the same curiosity. He reminded me of Jesus Christ dragging his cross!

We waited approximately fifteen minutes and he just sat there staring into the sky. Every now and then he stared at the crowd. Suddenly, he took his piano and dragged it away. People were silent and absorbed in their thoughts. The spot was empty in less than five minutes.

A week later on a Saturday morning, a beautiful summer day, lots of young people were dancing while skating. The park was crowded. I still recall, he was coming from Fifth Avenue towards the park dragging his piano on the street. Taxi drivers were screaming terrible names at him because he was obstructing the road. He looked so bony and mistreated, so sad and gloomy. He walked straight to the Washington Square Monument and placed his piano in the shade. He opened the piano cover and took a small stool out. People started to gather around him. Many of the expressions on people's faces were saying "What a weirdo!" People were always curious; so was I.

The speechless man looked around, sat on his stool and stared for a while. People continued to get closer, waiting for him to start. The crowd grew quite large. Suddenly, the man took a step from his stool and bowed, as if his performance were about to begin! Then he sat down and everyone laughed when he pulled his imaginary tuxedo tails from under his rear. His face remained serious, hands in position ready to begin his concert. "Why doesn't he start?" many of us wondered. "What is the problem?" Students were laughing and making fun of him. Others waited silently and shushed everyone to be quiet.

The man began to play. His dirty hands moved incredibly fast and smoothly on the piano keys. He played like a virtuoso. Total silence overtook the park. Everyone listened to the classical concerto played by the homeless man. No expression on his face, no smiles, only total concentration. His movements followed the rhythm of the melody. He was in a total trance with his music. We stood there in amazement, enjoying the beauty of his music. He played for an hour. It was great! When he stopped, people were shouting "Bravo, Bravo, Bravo!"

The applause wouldn't stop. People went on clapping, whistling and acknowledging him. Then he stood up from the tiny, insignificant stool and beamed with the most satisfied smile you could ever imagine. He was in ecstasy and so were we. People began to take dollars out of their wallets and place the money inside the piano cover. There was money all over the place.

Methodically, he folded his stool and placed it inside the piano, grabbed his chain and dragged the piano away. People asked him to play another piece, but he had played enough for one day. As he walked away, people were still applauding. I was pleased to see him sauntering away with the most fitting expression of accomplishment on his face. God bless his hands!

One thing continued to puzzle me. What was the true story behind this homeless virtuoso? I was so curious that I asked the deli owner about him. He told me that the only time he had ever heard the man utter a word, he had said, "I have no worries in the world. The sky is my roof, the earth is my bed, I've got plenty to eat and most importantly, I have my precious piano with me."

I. Response Journal

After reading the story, work with the Response Journal Questions. Share your answers in small groups. Each group will select one question and discuss the response with the class.

1. How did you feel about street people before you read the story? Did your opinion change after you read the story?

_____

_____

_____

2. Have you ever had an experience with a street person? If not, tell the group about an experience someone you know may have had.

_____

_____

_____

3. What do you think about the virtuoso's attitude towards life?

_____

_____

_____

_____

_____

4. Briefly describe your attitude towards life.

_____

_____

_____

_____

_____

_____

5. If you had been in the audience when the virtuoso performed, how would you have acted? Would you have approached him or would you have kept away? Explain your answer.

_____

_____

_____

_____

II. Mapping the Story

Use the chart below to map out the story. Show how we find out about the homeless man throughout the story. Indicate in which part of the plot each kind of characterization is used. In groups of three, compare and discuss the story map. In whole-class discussion, come to a consensus for each item on the chart.

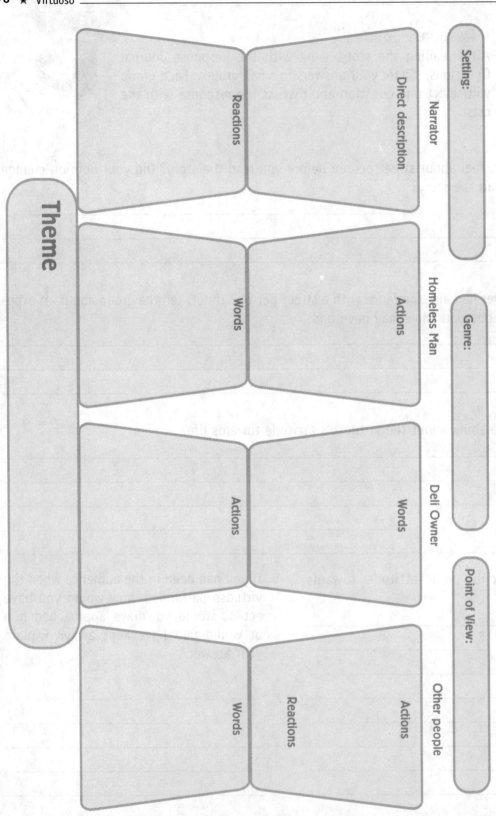

Setting:

Genre:

Point of View:

Narrator
Direct description
Reactions

Homeless Man
Actions
Words

Deli Owner
Words
Actions

Other people
Actions
Reactions
Words

Theme

III. Comprehension Questions

1. Describe the homeless man.

_____

_____

_____

2. What did the deli owner do every morning?

_____

_____

_____

3. Were people afraid of the homeless man? If so, why?

_____

_____

_____

4. What did the man do in the park?

_____

_____

_____

_____

5. How did people react after he played the piano?

_____

_____

_____

_____

6. Why doesn't he have any worries in his life?

_____

_____

_____

_____

IV. Looking More Closely

1. What do you think happened to this man?

_____

_____

_____

2. Why is his piano so important to him?

_____

_____

_____

_____

3. Why do you think the deli owner treats him so well?

_____

_____

_____

_____

V. Reflecting Further on the Story

Form groups of three or four. Discuss the following questions and present your answers to the class.

1. What would you say are the five main causes of homelessness? Do you think the majority of homeless people are mentally ill? Why or why not?

_____

_____

_____

2. What do you think can be done about the problem of homeless people? What can you do to help the homeless? Explain.

_____

_____

_____

3. If you were the president of your country, how would you help homeless people?

_____

_____

_____

4. Do you think discrimination against the homeless exists in your country? Can we link discrimination to homelessness? List the types of discrimination you are familiar with. Have you ever experienced discrimination? Explain.

_____

_____

_____

VI. Springboard

Going Beyond
Work with a partner. Select a country from the list below.

Go to the library or use other sources available to you to find information about homelessness in that country. You may want to look in magazines, encyclopedias, newspapers or the Internet. Present your findings to the class.

Mexico	The Dominican Republic	The United States	Britain
China	Brazil	Russia	

Different Perspectives
The teacher will show or assign the movie entitled *With Honors* in which Joe Pesci plays a homeless man. After viewing the movie, answer the following questions and prepare to discuss them in class.

1. Why is the role of the homeless man so significant?

_____

_____

2. What do the Harvard students learn from this homeless man?

_____

_____

_____

3. Why is it a mistake for the Harvard students to stereotype the homeless man?

_____

_____

_____

4. List examples of discrimination against the homeless man in the movie.

_____

_____

_____

Further Research: Welfare

Find information about the financial aid program in the United States, also known as the "Welfare Program to Help the Needy." Answer the questions below. Be prepared to discuss them in class.

1. Who invented welfare? What was its original purpose?

_____

_____

_____

2. Why hasn't welfare solved the problem of homelessness?

_____

_____

_____

3. What are some of the problems welfare is confronting today?

_____

_____

_____

On Your Own

If you know a homeless person in your community, write about him or her. Explain why the person became homeless or what the person's life is like. Read the story to the class. If you don't know a homeless person, write about what you think it would be like to be homeless.

_____

_____

_____

8. Lumpy Soup

On Your Own

Answer the following questions. Share your answers with the class.

1. We all have a favorite dish and a dish we dislike most. Do you remember what dish you hated as a child? Describe it. Explain why you hated it.

   _____

   _____

2. As a child, were you ever forced to eat something you really disliked? Who forced you to eat it? How did you feel being forced to eat it?

   _____

   _____

3. Do you believe older brothers and sisters should share in the responsibility of caring for their younger siblings? Why? Why not?

   _____

   _____

4. Do you think that sometimes adults forget what it was like to be a child? Explain your answer.

   _____

   _____

Make Your Prediction

Based on the above questions, what do you think this story will be about?
Try to guess who the characters will be.

_____

_____

_____

Lumpy Soup

Rosa Vallejo

We had never seen anything like it. Our bowls sat in front of us filled to the brim with a warm, thick, greenish-white liquid. My little brother looked at me with tears in his eyes.

"You have to eat it," I said. "If you don't, they won't give us any lunch tomorrow." He stared at the bowl again. I picked up my spoon and took a deep breath. I was older and had to set an example.

Everyone always told me this. "You are older," they said. "You are a big girl now." And it was true. I was already in second grade and William was only in kindergarten. I had to make sure we didn't get off the free lunch list. I knew it was my responsibility. I was older.

As the mysterious-looking liquid invaded my mouth, I could feel small lumps against my tongue. The taste was slightly salty but otherwise flat-not spicy like the food I was used to. I swallowed the lumpy liquid trying hard not to make a face so that I would be convincing to my brother.

"What does it taste like?"

"It's not bad," I lied.

"Does it taste like *sopón de gallina*?"

We both hated *sopón de gallina,* the thick rice soup made with the meat of a fresh young hen that we were forced to eat every Saturday. My father insisted it would keep us healthy.

"Oh, no. It doesn't. Really, it doesn't."

I wasn't lying as I said this, but I felt as if I were because the soup tasted even worse. One of the lunchroom matrons walked toward us. These ladies patrolled the area like wardens. My heart started pounding and I quickly gulped down another spoonful of the thick gruel. She came over and peered at our bowls. My heart was about to come out of my chest. She looked at my brother. He stared back at her and another tear rolled down his cheek. I desperately banged away at his skinny leg with my skinny leg under the table but he wouldn't get the hint. He never even picked up his spoon. The lady looked at him again, this time with a shadow of concern on her face.

"Why, what's wrong, honey?" she cooed. "Don't you like your soup?" I was astounded by the softness in her voice.

"No," my brother whimpered, sadly shaking his face from side to side. My heart almost gave out.

"Well, sweetie, just eat your sandwich. Okay? Oh, and drink your milk like a good little boy."

The smile on my brother's face was the broadest I'd ever seen. My pounding heart started to slow down and, when the lady turned to me, I was already putting my spoon down with relief. I too was ready with a smile.

The lady peered at my bowl again. "Well," she said, "I see you have started to eat your potato soup." The tone of her voice had lost its softness. "Now finish it up! You are older, and big girls like you know that we can't waste food. Think of all the starving children in the world!"

My heart dropped. I lowered my eyes and picked up my spoon. The words "potato soup" kept racing through my head. I had never heard of such a thing!

I opened my mouth, put in the spoon, and as I felt the lumpy texture of the soup on my tongue, I said a silent prayer. "Papa Dios," I prayed, "don't let me throw up. Please remember: I am older."

I. Response Journal

After reading the story, work with the Response Journal Questions. Share your answers in small groups. Each group will select one question and discuss the response with the class.

1. How do you feel about forcing children to eat something?

_____

_____

_____

2. What do you think about telling children to finish their food because of all the starving people in the world?

_____

_____

_____

3. Which character could you identify with more, the brother or the sister? Why?

_____

_____

_____

_____

_____

4. What do you think about the lunchroom matron's attitude toward the children?

_____

_____

_____

_____

_____

_____

5. What other issues, besides the children actually finishing the soup, do you think were involved in this situation?

_____

_____

_____

_____

_____

II. Mapping the Story

Use the chart below to map out the story. Show how the conflicts of each character are related to the theme of the story. In groups of three, compare and discuss the story map. In whole-class discussion, come to a consensus for each item on the chart.

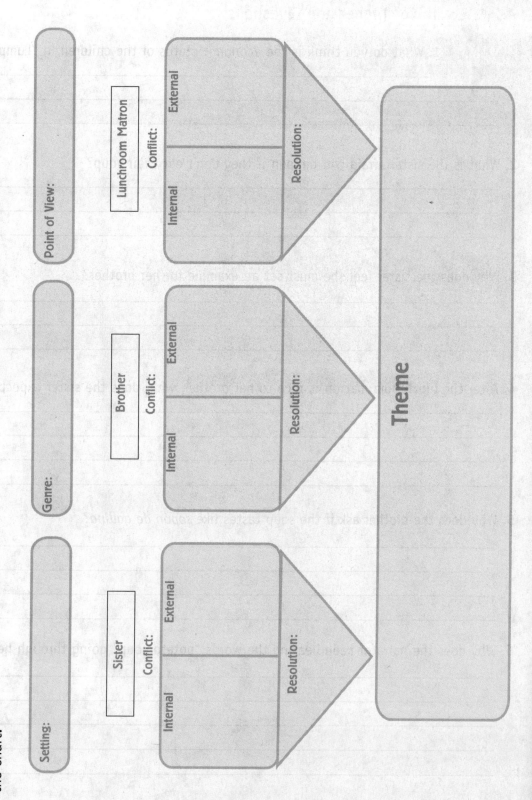

III. Comprehension Questions

1. What do you think is the economic status of the children in "Lumpy Soup"?

_____

_____

_____

2. What is the sister afraid will happen if they don't eat their soup?

_____

_____

_____

3. Why does the sister feel she must set an example for her brother?

_____

_____

_____

4. After the lunchroom matron is nice to her brother, what does the sister expect from her?

_____

_____

_____

_____

5. Why does the brother ask if the soup tastes like _sopón de gallina_?

_____

_____

_____

_____

6. Why does the narrator keep hearing the words "potato soup" going through her head?

_____

_____

_____

_____

IV. Springboard

Expressing Your Views
On your own, answer the following questions. Share your answers with the class.

1. If you had been the lunchroom matron, would you have treated the children differently? Write what you would have done.

2. How old do you think the narrator was? Do you think she should have felt so responsible for her brother? What do you think her parents might have told her about the free lunch program? Write down your ideas.

Analyzing the Issues
Work together. Select two of the following questions and follow the directions given for each one.

1. In small groups, discuss the following questions and share your ideas. Write down what you consider to be the best ideas. Be prepared to present them to the class.

   a. Do you think that sometimes adults put too much pressure on young children by giving them responsibilities that are beyond their capacity? What effects might this have on a young child?

   b. How much and what kind of responsibilities do you believe children should be expected to handle?

c. In your opinion, at what age should parents give responsibilities to their children?

_____

_____

_____

_____

2. Do you think the behavior that adults expect from young children is affected by culture? By economic status?

a. Do you think that in some cultures adults expect more responsible behavior from young children than in others?

_____

_____

_____

_____

b. Do you think that socioeconomic status affects the responsibilities parents give to their children?

_____

_____

_____

_____

Find information about how children live in different countries. How different or how similar are the lives of children in these countries? You can choose a country from the list below or select any other country you are interested in. You may want to look in magazines or journals, newspapers, textbooks, current encyclopedias or the Internet. If there are people from other countries in your community, you may wish to interview them.

China	England	Colombia	Mexico
India	Spain	Brazil	Puerto Rico

Does it make a big difference in the lives of these children if they come from rich or poor homes?

In groups, share the information you have found. Prepare an oral presentation for the class.

4. With a partner or in small groups, draw up what you consider would be a fair "Bill of Rights" for children. What things do you believe all children are entitled to? Share these with the class. Find the United Nation's Bill of Rights for children. Compare the ideas presented in the different documents.

9. The Latin Alien

Take a Stand

Answer the following questions. Share your answers with the class.

Do you believe in aliens? Do they or don't they exist?

Form two groups. If you believe aliens exist, join group A. If you believe aliens do not exist, join group B.

You will have approximately five minutes to work with your group and discuss opinions about the existence of aliens.

Appoint a secretary to write the reasons for your opinion on the chart provided on the following page. An oral debate will follow with the teacher as the moderator.

Group A: Yes, aliens do exist.

Group B: No, aliens do not exist.

On Your Own

Answer the following questions and discuss in class.

1. Would you go to the moon if tickets were being sold?
   Why or why not?

_____

_____

_____

_____

_____

Predict

2. What do you think the conflict in the story will be?

_____

_____

_____

_____

_____

Activity

Do you believe in aliens?

Group A: Yes _____   Group B: No _____

List your reasons.

1. _____

2. _____

3. _____

4. _____

5. _____

6. _____

7. _____

8. _____

9. _____

10. _____

The Latin Alien

Terry Mezo

Doña Leonides lives in the town of Aguas Buenas, Puerto Rico, located up in the central hills of the island. Many people know about this town because recently it has been the focus of news reports. Many people from there claim to have seen the goat-sucking monster more commonly known as the *chupacabras*. Canovanas is another town that has been a victim of these beings. Many people claim that at night these ugly-looking creatures kill domestic animals.

Last month, Leonides lost twenty rabbits and about ten chickens. Mr. Joaquín, her neighbor, lost eight goats, fifteen rabbits and some chickens, too. Many domestic animals have died in the claws of these monsters. The only strange clue left on the dead animals are two perforations similar to the ones vampires leave on their victims.

No one has been lucky enough to catch one of these slimy, sly creatures, yet many people claim to have seen them. Everyone is watching out for them. Many people have suffered sleepless nights because of these strange happenings. Some people say the government doesn't want to release information on the matter, but many cases have been reported and presented on TV, and even covered on the "Mystery Files" show. Other people say these creatures must be aliens. For the last twenty years or more, people have been claiming to have had encounters of the first, second or even third kind with these creatures. In fact, on a recent talk show a man insisted that he had had direct communication with an alien. Who knows what else people will come up with?

It's Thursday evening and Leonides turns on the TV to watch the news. The latest release is that some engineer from New York has disappeared in El Yunque rain forest. What could have happened to this man? How did he get lost? God only knows! Ms. Leonides is sure that these creatures have something to do with this missing man. She knows the alien headquarters have been established at the very top of El Yunque.

Panic invades her and immediately she starts closing all the windows in her house. She suddenly hears strange noises coming from outside, bushes moving and animals crying. "Dear God, protect us from these strange evils," she prays, shivering. She has her rosary made of little white beads hanging from her neck. Believing this will protect her from all evil somehow eases her mind.

Feeling very tense, she sits on her sofa, listening carefully to the experts on aliens on TV, who assure everyone that this lost tourist was abducted. Three days have gone by and there is still no trace or sign of life from the tourist. Leonides knows that there have been reports of people who have disappeared in this dark, sinister forest in the past.

Tania, Leonides' niece, who is about nineteen years old, walks in through the front door having just heard the news about the missing tourist. She says, "If this man was on his way to Mt. Britton, which is approximately an hour and a half's walk, something must have caught his attention to pull him away from the crowd. Why didn't he follow the paths made by the people that walk to the top? I'm sure he was up to no good. Either that or he had too many piña coladas before he started his journey."

"Tania," Leonides says in a demanding voice, "please don't joke about this. It's a serious matter."

Tania ignores her aunt and quickly walks out the door.

***

A week has gone by and Leonides has not missed the news for any reason. She doesn't know the missing man, but prays for him. She goes to sleep and every now and then opens an eye and tunes in her ears to the noises of the night.

It's 5:00 p.m. Monday, time for the Channel 2 news. She's not really interested in the political gossip. She's just wondering about…Yes! The lost tourist appeared! He is in terrible shape, speechless, with long hair and heavy beard, sunburned, barefoot, and shaky. News reporters inform the public that he has been driven to the local hospital. The man has lost about thirty-five pounds in twelve days.

"What happened?" ask the reporters.

And Mr. Whipple replies, "I got lost. The group I was with was walking too fast. I slowed down and lost track of them."

"Why did you keep going up?" inquire the reporters. "Why didn't you follow the streams downhill?"

During the interview, the tourist is in a total daze and seems completely spaced out. The look in his eyes projects fear and confusion. He only utters a few statements. He says that "El Yunkay," as he pronounces it, was terribly cold at night, and he had to eat ferns, worms, mushrooms and bananas, if he found any, to survive. The *coquís* did not allow him to sleep at all and it rained every single night. He saw strange little lights flickering in the dark. Finally, he says that the worst nightmare was the mystifying blackness of the forest. Before saying good-bye he says he will be back to write about his experience in the rain forest.

Leonides sighs with relief, " Hmm ... I know this man saw aliens up there."

The following week a group of tourists who are hiking in the forest disappear for three days. They appear somewhere in Gurabo, on the other side of the gigantic Yunque mountain. They can't explain how they got lost, but are pretty happy about their "transcendental experience."

Leonides is sure that these people were in search of an alien encounter.

"When, when will this puzzle be solved?" Leonides wonders.

Tania drops in to ask Leonides if she has heard the news about the lost and found tourist group. "Those people were probably on drugs, hallucinating or drinking too much!" says Tania.

"What's the problem with you?" Leonides exclaims. "You think the only thing people do is drink? Take something seriously for once in your life!"

Tania quickly walks out the door. "See ya," she says. She loves to aggravate her aunt.

Knowing that the tourists are safe, the next morning Leonides wakes up feeling happy. "What a beautiful day! I'm going to plant some tomato seeds!" And out the door she walks with the seeds in her hands. After working in the yard for three hours, she takes a nap in her hammock.

Later on, when she wakes up and goes into the house to start dinner, she turns on the TV and hears, "Tonight on 'It Happened Like This,' don't miss the latest reports on the *chupacabras* that has just arrived in Mexico." This special edition reported one curious detail: "No English-speaking persons have reported encounters with this strange creature."

Leonides opens her eyes in total disbelief! She is so happy because these aliens have taken a plane to another country, meaning she will finally get her full night's sleep. For a minute she thinks, "These creatures must really like warm-blooded Latinos! No Americans have seen them yet! Why Spanish–speaking people only?"

I. Response Journal

After reading the story, work with the Response Journal
Questions. Share your answers in small groups. Each group
will select one question and discuss the response with the
class.

1. How do you feel about the title of the story?

_____

_____

_____

2. Have you ever had an experience with an alien? If not, write about an experience someone you know has had or one you are familiar with from a book or movie.

_____

_____

_____

3. What do you think of Leonides? Why do you think she is so interested in the aliens?

_____

_____

_____

_____

4. How would you react in this situation?

_____

_____

_____

_____

_____

_____

_____

5. What do you think about the way the
   subject of aliens is handled in the story?
   How realistic do you think it is?

_____

_____

_____

_____

_____

_____

_____

II. Mapping the Story

Use the chart below to map out the story. Show how the descriptions of the setting and the stereotypical attitudes of the characters affect the atmosphere. In groups of three, compare and discuss the story map. In whole-class discussion, come to a consensus for each item on the chart.

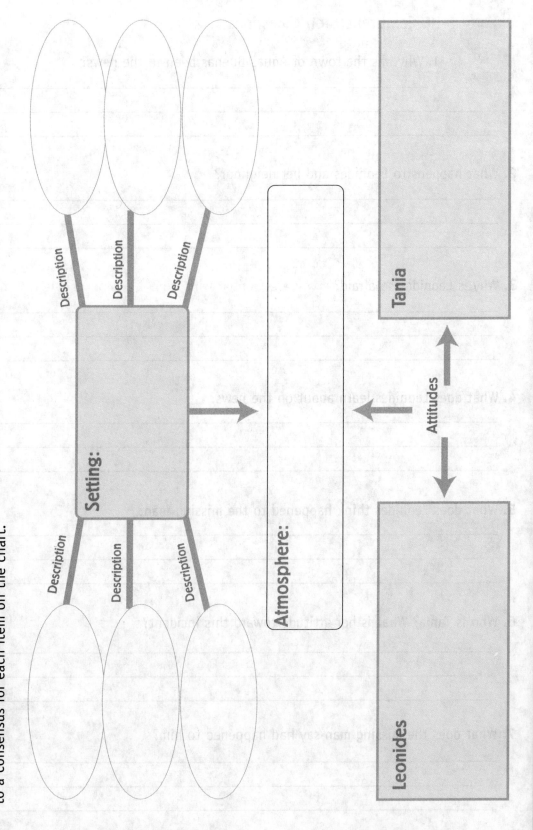

III. Comprehension Questions

1. Why has the town of Aguas Buenas been in the news?

_____

_____

_____

2. What happens to Leonides and her neighbor?

_____

_____

_____

3. Why is Leonides so afraid?

_____

_____

_____

4. What does Leonides learn about on the news?

_____

_____

_____

5. What does Leonides think happened to the missing man?

_____

_____

_____

6. Who is Tania? What is her attitude toward this incident?

_____

_____

_____

7. What does the missing man say had happened to him?

_____

_____

_____

8. What country did the creatures reappear in?

_____

_____

_____

_____

IV. Looking More Closely

1. What do you think is causing domestic animals to die in the story?

_____

_____

_____

2. How would you describe Leonides?

_____

_____

_____

3. Have you ever been to a rain forest? If you have, describe the experience of going up, the surroundings, and the weather.

_____

_____

_____

_____

4. Do you think rain forests are dangerous places?

_____

_____

_____

5. Where do you think aliens would hide?

_____

_____

V. Reflecting Further on the Story

Work with a partner. Select one of the questions below. Be prepared to discuss your answers orally.

1. Do you think the government would hide information regarding UFO's (unidentified flying objects) and the existence of aliens? Discuss.

_____

_____

_____

2. If aliens existed, would you like to have an encounter with one? Explain.

_____

_____

_____

3. If you were the owner of a farm and all your animals died mysteriously, as happened to Leonides and Joaquín one night, what do you think your immediate reaction would be?

_____

_____

_____

4. Are humans ready to share the universe with other creatures? Explain.

_____

_____

_____

VI. Springboard

Assessing the Topic

1. Work with a partner. Choose a movie related to the topic of aliens. Give a brief oral summary about the movie you choose. Don't forget to answer "who, what, where, when, why" and "how" questions about the movie. You can also use the story map form as a guide to prepare your summary.

Suggested movies:

The Day the Earth Stood Still	E.T.	The Arrival
Mars Attack	Resurrection	Men in Black
Fire in the Sky	Star Wars	Species
Roswell	Lost in Space	X Files
Alien	Contact	Event Horizon
Independence Day		

Linking the Topic

Think about children's cartoons today and toys based on the characters. Do you think the physical appearance of these toys will affect children's concept of beauty? Following are some examples of cartoons children watch. Describe the appearance of the characters and your opinion on the matter.

Teenage Mutant Ninja Turtles   Ren and Stimpy
Beavis and Butthead   Gargoyles

_____

_____

_____

_____

_____

Surveying

You are going to work on a survey. Ask five children from your neighborhood whether or not they believe in aliens. In class, you will divide yourselves into groups of five and discuss your findings from the survey. You will work with your group to make a chart that illustrates the findings.

_____

_____

_____

_____

_____

10. The Menorah

On Your Own

Answer the following questions. Share your answers with your classmates.

1. In you own words, define the word "prejudice."

_____

_____

_____

2. When was the first time you became aware that there were different races, religions and cultures?

_____

_____

_____

3. Was there ever a time that you felt you had to dislike someone because your family or friends did?

_____

_____

_____

4. How would you feel if someone were prejudiced against you because of your religion or ethnic background?

_____

_____

_____

Collaborating

These symbols represent some of the religions of the world. With a partner, try to match each symbol to a religion. Write the name of the religion under the symbol that represents it.

1. _____ 2. _____ 3. _____ 4. _____ 5. _____

Select from these religions: Christianity, Hinduism, Islam, Judaism, Taoism

The Menorah

Rosa A. Vallejo

There were only two third-grade classes and Amelia´s group was the lucky one because they had Miss Goldman for a teacher. No one liked the other teacher, Mrs. Kane. She was really mean. Sometimes, even with the door of her classroom closed, her voice could be heard yelling at her students to behave. Miss Goldman never yelled. She always had a smile on her face. All the kids loved her and were never afraid of her the way they were of Mrs. Kane. Sometimes just seeing Mrs. Kane walking down the hall made the students stand straight and hold their breath. But Miss Goldman only made them want to run to her and hug her.

Amelia felt especially lucky and happy because inside of herself she was sure that she was Miss Goldman's favorite. Miss Goldman was nice to all the students, and everyone had a special job to do for her, but she would always ask Amelia to be in charge when she had to leave the room. When something had to be taken to the office it was usually Amelia who was asked to go.

Miss Goldman often told the kids things about herself. They knew that the beautiful ring on the finger of her left hand meant that she was getting married soon. And they knew that the man she was going to marry was named Mr. Birnbaum. Amelia loved to think of Miss Goldman in a wedding gown, walking down the aisle of the church. Sometimes she even imagined that she was a part of the wedding.

One day just before Christmas vacation, Miss Goldman brought a beautiful silver candelabra to school. It was decorated with a star that seemed to be made up of two triangles, one pointing up and one pointing down. She placed it on her desk and then wrote a word on the blackboard. It was a strange and long word, and although Amelia tried to sound it out in her head, it was very difficult.

"Today I am going to tell you about Hanukkah," Miss Goldman said. "Hanukkah is a special holiday that Jewish people celebrate. This year we will be celebrating it next week while many of you will be celebrating Christmas."

"I didn't know she was Jewish," the girl next to Amelia whispered.

Amelia just stared at her, but she felt a little uncomfortable. The way the girl had said "Jewish" made it sound like something bad.

"Don't you know what that means?" her classmate asked, looking a little surprised at Amelia.

"Know what?" Amelia asked, but she was afraid. She didn't really want to know anything that might make Miss Goldman not perfect.

"They were mean to Jesus! They don't like him!"

Amelia sucked in her breath. "I never heard that before," she whispered with as much emphasis as she could.

"Well," said her classmate, "if you don't believe me, ask your mother or the religion teacher. It's in the Bible, you know."

"Girls," Miss Goldman interrupted them. "Do you have a question?"

Both girls shook their heads. Amelia's heart was pounding. How could Miss Goldman be part of the people who had killed Jesus? Amelia loved Jesus. She was learning about Him in her religion class. No one else at home was very interested in religion or going to church, but she was. She loved learning about God and how much He loved her, and she especially loved learning about Jesus. She was very fond of the sweet Baby Jesus that Mary held in her arms at Christmas, and she felt very bad for the grown-up Jesus who died on the cross. It was such a terrible way to die. She thought about the awful nails going into His hands. She had seen a movie where they showed that once. Just thinking about it made her feel like crying.

"Would you like to come up and touch the menorah?" Miss Goldman sounded far away. "Just come up one by one."

Amelia could not move. She felt like she had butterflies in her stomach, and she could feel her heart pounding in her ears. She was afraid to look at the teacher. Everyone else went up, even the girl who had told her about the teacher being Jewish. She knew she would hurt Miss Goldman's feelings if she didn't touch the menorah. She really loved Miss Goldman, but now she didn't know if that was right. Was it all right to love Miss Goldman even if she was Jewish? If the Jewish people were mean to Jesus, did that mean that Miss Goldman was happy about those terrible things they had done to Jesus in the movie?

"Aren't you coming up, Amelia?" the teacher asked.

Amelia hesitated. Then she took one step towards the teacher's desk, but she just couldn't make herself go any closer. Instead, she asked if she could go to the bathroom.

★★★

Amelia stared out at the cold January day. The day before, everyone in class had made snowflakes out of white paper and the teacher had taped them to the window-panes. Now Amelia had to look between them, or through the holes made by their intricate patterns to make out the empty school yard outside. She couldn't concentrate on the math problems she was supposed to be doing, and she wanted the day to go fast so that she could leave the classroom. She didn't feel like being there anymore.

When she had asked her mother about Jesus and the Jewish people, Amelia had been astounded to learn that Jesus was Jewish Himself. Her mother had told her that being Jewish meant that you had a different way of worshipping God, and besides that, Miss Goldman had nothing to do with what had happened to Jesus. Still, Amelia could not feel the same about her class.

Even though Miss Goldman was still the nicest teacher in third grade, and was still nice to her, Amelia always had an uncomfortable feeling when she thought about the day of the menorah. She had never deliberately hurt anyone's feelings before, and yet she had not been able to stop herself that day. Now she felt sad, as if she had lost something that day, but she just wasn't sure exactly what it was. Sometimes she even wished that Miss Goldman were mean the way Mrs. Kane was. Then maybe she wouldn't feel so bad about having hurt her feelings.

"Why did she ever have to bring that menorah anyway?" she asked herself as she looked at the clock at the front of the room. "If she hadn't brought the menorah to school, things would still be the same." She sighed and went back to her math problems. There were so many hours still to go.

I. Response Journal

After reading the story, work with the Response Journal Questions. Share your answers in small groups. Each group will select one question and discuss the response with the class.

1. What was your reaction to the title "The Menorah"?

_____

_____

_____

2. Do you think Amelia really offended Miss Goldman? Why or why not? Have you ever seriously hurt a person you cared about?

_____

_____

_____

3. Was Amelia's conflict resolved? What would you say to her to make her feel more comfortable?

_____

_____

_____

_____

4. What do you think about the way Miss Goldman handled the presentation of the menorah?

_____

_____

_____

_____

_____

_____

5. Have you ever been in a situation where you felt strange because everyone else was from a different nationality or religion?

_____

_____

_____

_____

_____

_____

II. Mapping the Story

Use the chart below to map out the story. Show how different resolutions to Amelia's conflict would change the theme. In groups of three, compare and discuss the story map. In whole-class discussion, come to a consensus for each item on the chart.

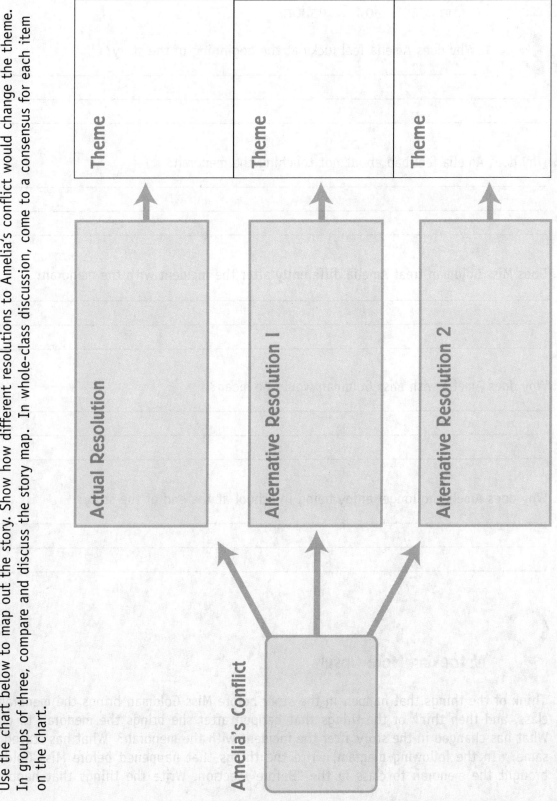

III. Comprehension Questions

1. Why does Amelia feel lucky at the beginning of the story?

_____

_____

2. Why does Amelia feel bad about not touching the menorah?

_____

_____

3. Does Miss Goldman treat Amelia differently after the incident with the menorah?

_____

_____

4. Why does Amelia wish Miss Goldman would be mean?

_____

_____

5. Why does Amelia no longer enjoy being in school at the end of the story?

_____

_____

IV. Looking More Closely

1. Think of the things that happen in the story before Miss Goldman brings the menorah to class, and then think of the things that happen after she brings the menorah to class. What has changed in the story after the incident with the menorah? What has stayed the same? In the following diagram, write the things that happened before Miss Goldman brought the menorah to class in the "Before" section. Write the things that happened after the teacher brought the menorah to class in the "After" section. In the intersection of the two sections write the things that stayed the same. Include the feelings of the characters in your lists.

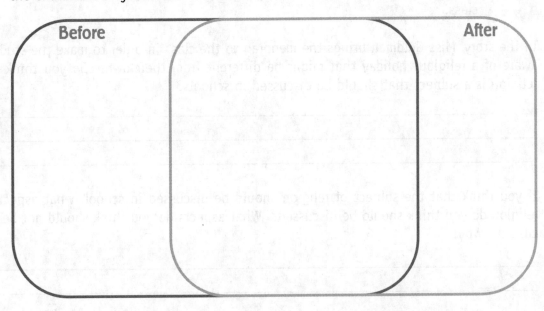

2. Discuss the following questions with a partner and come to an agreement for each answer.

a. When Amelia imagines Miss Goldman walking down the aisle, what has she assumed about Miss Goldman?

_____

_____

b. Why do you think Amelia's classmate makes such a point of telling Amelia that Miss Goldman is Jewish? What do you think it means to her? Where might she have gotten her ideas?

_____

_____

c. Why is Amelia so confused?

_____

_____

d. Why does Amelia say that she wishes the teacher had never brought the menorah to school?

_____

_____

V. Springboard

Expressing Your Views

On your own, answer the following questions. Share your answers with the class.

1. In the story, Miss Goldman brings the menorah to the class in order to make the students aware of a religious holiday that might be different from their own. Do you think that religion is a subject that should be discussed in schools?

_____

_____

_____

2. If you think that the subject of religion should be discussed in school, what aspects of religion do you think should be discussed? What aspects do you think should not be discussed. Why?

_____

_____

_____

3. If you don't think religion should be discussed in schools, explain why.

_____

_____

_____

Bringing the Story to Your World

1. With a partner, find information about a religion other than your own. What holidays do the people in this religion observe? How do they observe them? Prepare an oral report based on this information. Perhaps you can find out if there are members of this religion living in your community.

_____

_____

_____

_____

_____

The Menorah ★ 113

_____

_____

_____

_____

2. With a partner, write a different ending for this story. First, brainstorm about the ideas you would change, and discuss why you would change them. You may wish to think about whether this story could happen today in your community. When you write the ending, you can write it as if it were happening today. Share your endings with the rest of the class, and be prepared to explain why you ended the story the way you did.

_____

_____

_____

_____

_____

_____

_____

_____

_____

Analyzing the Issues
Work together. Select two of the following questions and follow the directions given for each question.

1. In a small group, discuss the following questions. Write down your ideas, and be prepared to share them with the class.
   • Do you think prejudice is something we learn?

_____

_____

_____

_____

- What causes people to dislike those who are different from them?

  _____

  _____

  _____

- Do we have to develop our prejudices early in life, or can we develop prejudices at any age?

  _____

  _____

  _____

- Do you think we can get over our prejudice against those who are different from us in some way? How can we do this?

  _____

  _____

  _____

2. With a partner or in small groups talk about peer pressure. How much influence do your friends or classmates have on you? Have you ever done something to please your friends even though you knew it was wrong? Do you think that we are influenced by our peers at all ages, or do you think peer pressure only is an issue in childhood and adolescence? Share your ideas with the class.

  _____

  _____

  _____

  _____

  _____

  _____

11. Falling

Make your Prediction

This story is going to be about _____

_____

_____

_____

Answer and Discuss

1. Do you believe people can fall in love at first sight?

_____

_____

_____

2. Do you know anyone who has?

_____

_____

3. Where can you meet the ideal person to be your mate?

_____

_____

_____

4. Would you go out with someone your parents chose for you?

_____

_____

_____

Make a List

Work with a partner. Write a list of activities you consider to be fun for teenagers today.

1. _____
2. _____
3. _____
4. _____
5. _____
6. _____
7. _____

Falling

Terry Mezo

It was Ellen's second year at the university when Mark came along.

She was enjoying life, partying, studying, establishing priorities in order for all the important things in life to flow smoothly. She always respected her mother's philosophy of happiness.

"You must study hard," her mom would say, "but you must also party. Dance, make friends, and be responsible because all these things are necessary if you want a happy life. Balance. All extremes are dangerous." Ellen knew her mom was a wise woman and admired her for her qualities.

The library was the hangout. Between bookshelves Ellen and her friends chatted but also studied. Weekends were generally spent at Costa Azul in Luquillo. It was the favorite spot for enjoyment: playing paddleball, running free along the beach, sunbathing or listening to the ocean's mystifying secrets which sometimes sounded like angry uproars and other times like passive weeping. An interesting magazine to browse through, or a radio to listen to–the Stylistics, Elton John, Diana Ross, or Air Supply–was also entertaining. It was a close group of friends that gathered together on weekends for fun. The weekend was never long enough to do all the things they enjoyed. Monday was just around the corner. Nothing good lasts forever, it is said, and it was true.

Early Monday morning as she entered the library, there was this guy singing a strange song that evoked Ellen's name. She turned to the guy and asked..."What?"

The guy looked at her and said, "I'm just singing. Why?"

Ellen said, "I'm sorry, I thought you were calling my name."

The good-looking young guy with an attitude replied, "So, your name is Ellen," and continued his song.

Ellen thought, "What a jerk!" and kept on walking. Later, however, for some strange reason this guy started invading her dreams. She dreamt they were playing paddleball and racing each other to the other end of the beach.

Another weekend approached and the usual crowd planned their trip to the beach. Saturday turned out to be a perfect day with a clear blue sky and sea and a balmy breeze. The palms were swaying with the wind as if the wind carried some uplifting rhythm. Looking at them from one end of the beach to the other, the palms seemed like the Radio City Rockettes, all fronds moving in one direction, dancing to the rhythm of Willie Colon's music. There was rhythm in the wind–no doubt about it!

Ellen took a walk along the shore and from afar her attention was driven to this exquisitely handsome young man. He was nicely tanned with black, very black velvety hair, and a perfect body. The way his tan contrasted with the yellow creamy color of the sand was very attractive. She walked faster to see if she could catch up with him, but couldn't. He seemed to be in a hurry. Suddenly, he dropped his fins and snorkel and turned to pick them up. This gave Ellen a chance to catch up with him, and she stood there astonished when she realized that this "hunk" was the same guy that had been singing at the library. "Gosh! Swimsuits do make a difference," she thought. She snapped out of her trance and realized he had vanished, gone. Poof!

The following Monday Ellen went straight to the library to wait for her friends at the usual spot between the bookshelves. She selected a book and glanced at it, but a nicely tuned voice interrupted.

"Can I join you?"

Ellen looked up and there was the guy. "Okay," Ellen answered. Her heart was beating at 80 mph. She couldn't understand or control it.

"You look like one of those conceited chicks that gets very little done," he said.

"Excuse me," Ellen replied. "Is that the impression I give you? Well, you're in for a big surprise!" She felt he was judging her too fast. *Who does he think he is? He doesn't even know me*, she thought.

He kept trying to make conversation and after a while the tension wore down. They chatted about a lot of things. They talked about life, sports, music, classes and art. Art, indeed, was his favorite subject so they picked books and compared Michelangelo and Salvador Dali. He favored Dali. Later on, he stood up and said "I hate to go, but I've got a class. Nice talking to you. My name is Mark."

They got to know each other and for a while enjoyed each other's company. Then things turned out a little crazy. Mark started acting kind of nutty. One day when Ellen was walking through the hall on her way to class, he started screaming out in front of everyone, "Hey students! There goes the girl I'm going to marry!" Ellen's blood boiled; she was steaming with anger. She could feel blood flowing to her face. This was the most humiliating experience ever. She was shocked by his crazy attitude.

After that, every single day he would embarrass her by calling her name out loud in the hallway. He would shout to the students in the hall. "See that bad-tempered girl? The skinny, curly-headed one? She's gonna be mine."

This infuriated Ellen more and more to the point where her first impression about him went down the drain. He had seemed so nice at the library.

She thought to herself. "What a waste. Such a hunk turns out to be a loony". She felt embarrassed and uneasy, especially while walking the college grounds, not knowing when this loony would strike again. Sometimes when she would stop for a drink of water at the fountain, before she knew it, he was pressing the water button for her, saying things like "You're gonna marry me, you have no escape. I know it." Ellen would stand there speechless. She felt like killing him. People just laughed. They found his obsession quite amusing. Mark was very smart. He even started mingling with her friends and ended up in the same crowd.

One day the group planned a trip to a disco and Ellen didn't want to go. She knew he would find out about the trip and would show up at the place. "After all these humiliating scenes, I can't risk going if he is. He will ruin my night at the disco," she said to one of her friends.

Everyone already knew Mark would show up, but they told her that he had other plans. So Ellen decided to go.

The group agreed to meet at seven o'clock. Ellen was riding with Alex, Ruth, and Julio. The moment she got into the car, Mr. Mark appeared from nowhere with this big smile on his face, telling everyone to make room for him.

"Move over, I'm riding next to the curly one."

She was so furious, she didn't utter a word. She felt like a sardine in a can, because he was squashing her. A while after the car had taken off, Ellen asked Alex to please stop the car. Alex didn't like her tone so he ignored her.

"Stop the car NOW!" she said angrily. Alex sensed her anger and stopped the car immediately. She stepped out of the car and said, "Mark get out here! We need to talk! Who invited you? " He looked at her with these penetrating eyes that suddenly confused her. "Well?" she said. Before she knew it he was kissing her ...and what a kiss! She was floating in the air; she had lost perspective; she had drifted to the clouds; she had never felt anything like this before. "Oh! My God, what is happening?" she thought.

Calmly and gently, as if nothing had happened, Mark said, "Can we get into the car and continue to our destination?" Ellen was mute all the way to the disco. She pinched herself and didn't feel a thing. "WOW!" Ellen thought, "how different I feel! Mark, Mark, Mark," she kept repeating in her mind. "I like you Mark! But you are crazy!"

They arrived at the disco and it was very crowded. The music was great and they were ready to party. The group rapidly made it to the dance floor and danced the rest of the night. Ellen was on cloud nine all night!

She was so high up in the clouds that she kept stumbling on the dance floor. Her friends made fun of her all night. Every time they went near her they would say, "So he finally got you to fall."

✱✳✱

I. Response Journal

After reading the story, work with the Response Journal Questions. Share your answers in a small group. Each group will select one question and discuss the responses with the class.

1. Have you ever fallen in love? What happened? If not, how do you imagine it would be?

_____

_____

_____

_____

2. Did you expect Ellen to fall for Mark at the end of the story? Why or why not?

_____

_____

_____

3. How does this love story compare to others you have read or seen in the movies?

_____

_____

_____

4. How realistic do you think the story is? Explain.

_____

_____

_____

_____

_____

5. What do you think of Ellen's mother's recipe for a happy life? What is your recipe?

_____

_____

_____

_____

_____

II. Mapping the Story

Use the chart below to map out the story. How do the characters' thoughts, actions and words help move the plot along? Show the characterization of the main characters during each part of the plot. In one sentence, write what happens in each part of the story. Compare and discuss your story map with two or three classmates. In whole-class discussion, come to a consensus for each item on the chart.

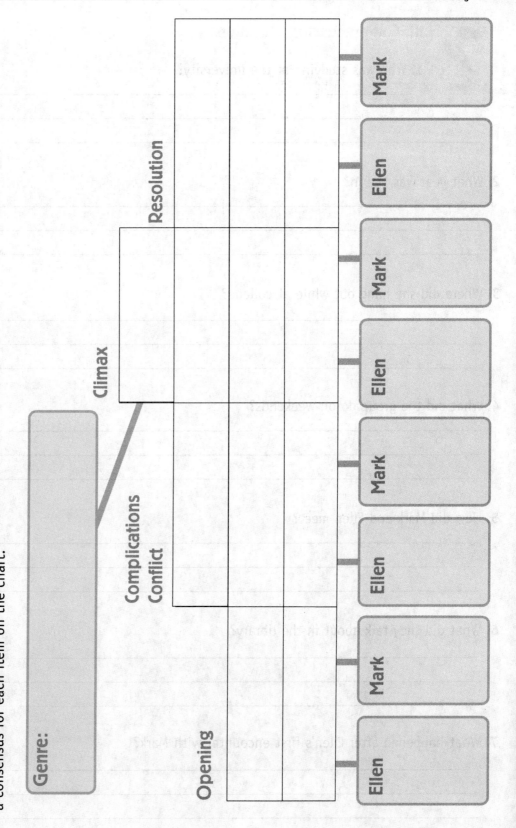

Genre:

Opening

Ellen Mark Ellen Mark

Complications
Conflict

Ellen Mark

Climax

Ellen Mark

Resolution

Ellen Mark

III. Comprehension Questions

1. Who was studying at the university?

2. What year was she in?

3. Where did she hang out while at college?

4. What did the group do on weekends?

5. How did Mark and Ellen meet?

6. What did they talk about in the library?

7. What happened after Ellen's first encounter with Mark?

8. Why did Ellen feel embarrassed?

_____

_____

9. Where were they going in the car?

_____

_____

_____

IV. Looking More Closely

1. What equilibrium is Ellen talking about?

_____

_____

_____

2. Do you believe this balance is necessary?

_____

_____

_____

3. How is university life different from high school?

_____

_____

_____

4. What kind of music do young people listen to?

_____

_____

_____

5. How are relationships different today from the time when the story takes place?

_____

_____

_____

6. What is your concept of "hangout"? What does it mean?

_____

_____

_____

7. Is Ellen in love? How do you know?

_____

_____

_____

8. Is Mark crazy? What is your opinion? Should she take him seriously?

_____

_____

_____

9. Do you think Ellen and Mark will marry?

_____

_____

_____

10. Why do you think clubs were referred to as discos?

_____

_____

_____

V. Reflecting Further on the Story

Work with a partner. Be prepared to share your answers with the class.

1. Write a different ending for the story.

_____

_____

_____

_____

_____

2. When do you consider someone a good friend?

_____
_____
_____

3. How long does it take to really know someone well?

_____
_____
_____

4. Do you think young people give themselves enough time to get to know each other?

_____
_____
_____

5. What do you think about dating people from other cultures?

_____
_____
_____

VI. Springboard
On Your Own

Work in groups of four. Discuss the questions below.
Select a student from the group to present your answers to the class.

1. At what age should teenagers start dating? Going to discos? Going alone to the movies? Are your views different from those of your parents?

_____
_____

2. What are some of the consequences of starting relationships too fast?

_____
_____

3. What do you think about dating games? Are they effective? Discuss.

_____

_____

4. You are going on a blind date. What are the first three questions you will ask your blind date?

a. _____

b. _____

c. _____

5. Give three reasons why you would break up with a person.

a. _____

b. _____

c. _____

6. Choose one of the following expressions and explain what it means to you.

a. Love is a lottery.

b. All that glitters is not gold.

c. Love is blind.

_____

_____

7. Complete this statement: The three most important things I look for in a date

are: _____ , _____ ,

and _____ .

8. Make a list of the ways in which the teenagers in the story enjoy their free time. Compare this list with your list from the pre-reading section. Discuss the similarities and differences.

Going Beyond

Choose a country of your preference and look for information about dating habits or marriage customs.

Prepare an oral presentation for the class.

12. The Camuy Caves

Collaborating

Work in groups of three or five to discuss the activities below. Be prepared to discuss your ideas with the class.

1. Brainstorming: List some sports you consider extremely dangerous.

_____   _____
_____   _____
_____   _____

2. Have you ever been hiking, scuba diving, camping, or rappelling?

_____
_____

Did you need special equipment? Was it exciting?

_____
_____

3. Would you like to climb Mount Everest or the Alps, go deep into the Amazon region, go sky diving, rappelling or bungee jumping?
Why or why not?

_____
_____
_____

4. Find information about some of these sports and discuss them with the group. You can search for information in sports magazines, newspaper articles, encyclopedias or the Internet.

The Camuy Caves

Terry Mezo

In memory of our beloved Thalia Veve.
This is a fictionalized version of events that actually occurred.

Puerto Rico is a miniature paradise. It is an island of great tourist attractions. Many beautiful beaches surround it. On the north, we have the Atlantic Ocean and on the south, the Caribbean Sea. A majestic chain of mountains runs through the very center of the island, beginning on the east and crossing all the way to the west. The sun can be extremely hot but a tropical breeze can always be felt under the palm trees. Many restaurants serve divine typical meals. The island has important historical landmarks that reveal its Spanish heritage–places such as El Morro, and the San Sebastian Castle. The Indian Park located in Utuado is representative of the indigenous Taíno culture. There is also great geological wealth. This can be especially appreciated in the Camuy River Cave Systems which are among its most important ecological systems. There are caves around this region that extend to the towns of Lares and Hatillo where small caves can be found too. They are a major tourist attraction on the island.

Norman Veve, a man of vast attributes, has dedicated a great deal of his life to investigating the natural riches of Puerto Rico. He is the precursor of the Speleology Association on the island. Exploring caves and studying their formation has been his hobby for many years. Thalia, his beautiful and timid daughter inherited the same interests. She was not very tall. Her complexion was soft and of a light-caramel tone. Her eyes projected a sweetness that, along with her humble smile, you could never forget. She shared so many of her father's hobbies that they became very close. More than a father and daughter, they were best friends. His other children enjoyed nature too, but Thalia was devoted to nature and exploring as much as her father was. Every weekend he and his children, Thalia, Tania, and Iván, in addition to a crew of friends brought together by the same interests and curiosity, would head for the mountains located in different towns of the small island to explore its caves. It is known that locals had already discovered some of the caves, but it was Norman who was among the first to truly explore them. Thalia designed and developed the first maps for these caves and for their subterranean water systems. Norman and Thalia shared a passion for the mysteries hidden in these caves, and looked foward to the challenges they might encounter in them.

On a Saturday morning during the month of June, the usual expedition crew gathered to continue tracing the underwater currents running through the Camuy Caves. They headed out to the Enchanted Cave, which is one of the largest in the system. Norman's friend, Nestor, showed up with his girlfriend. He had missed several of the previous expeditions, but he did not want to miss this one. Everyone was well equipped, carrying backpacks, helmets, water, ropes, flashlights, canned food, and diving gear as well as cameras and lighting equipment for photography. Thalia, with her note pad and her measuring device ready for jotting down descriptive details to help her draw her maps, carefully followed the crew. They were so heavily equipped and excited one would have thought they were headed for the moon.

They began their hike. From the main road to the cave it was about a two or three hour walk. At the entrance of this cave, Norman said, "Hey, guys. We're gonna have to cross this deep underground river to surface on the other side of the cave."

The water was so clear and cold. They rapidly put on their scuba diving equipment and began to dive in. They followed each other slowly, using their water flashlights to avoid getting lost. Thalia was appreciating the beauty of the blind albino fish that live in total darkness and have no sight.

They all made it safe and sound to the other side. The area they reached was totally dark. Because the sun's rays couldn't be felt and the temperature had been steadily dropping, some of the crew members were shivering. Once they had set up the lighting system, they all looked up at the same time and were mesmerized by the gigantic stalactites, which looked like enormous popsicles hanging from the top. They were also surrounded by stalagmites that seemed to be melting into the floor. Thalia recognized the strong odor of *guano* and said, "Dad, I smell bat droppings in here. That means there is another way into the cave because we know bats can't swim."

"You're right," Norman replied. "Let's find that entrance."

After a few hours in the cave, they found a smaller cave with its own lake running through it. It was impressive. Nestor said, "Let's baptize this cave after you. Norman's Cave it shall be officially called."

They were having a good time and hours passed unnoticed. The silence and the calm water made them feel as if they were in another world where there was no sense of time. But before they knew it, it was 5:00 p.m. Norman's eyes were fixed on the water when suddenly he realized that the water level was rising.

"Crew, we must get out of here immediately! Now! Move it! We can't exit the cave now, so run to the highest points. It seems a flash flood is coming down. If it is pouring outside, the water levels in here could rise extremely high. Our lives are in danger!"

The crew divided into two groups, but everyone was holding on to one rope just in case the strong water currents pulled them apart.

"Stay where you are," Norman repeated to the crew. "Don't try... Don't try to cross over because if the current runs wild it will catch you halfway. We're in danger anyway, but stay put."

Nestor started getting anxious because his girlfriend was with the other group. When Norman glanced over he had already started to cross.

"Go back! Go back!" Norman yelled. When Norman looked again, tons of water were coming down. Nestor was carried away by the furious waters.

The others all stood there in mute shock! The currents were flowing for about two hours. Then the water level went back down. They were speechless, crying, and confused. On their way back they searched for Nestor but had no luck. They only found his helmet.

❂❂❂

Two weeks had passed and the group had not met. One day Norman, their leader, called a meeting for 7:00 p.m. They would meet at the usual place.

Norman was preparing to deliver his message. He stood there silently for ten seconds, then said, "I know we all miss Nestor a lot. I know ... I do. He was a very special person, one who admired nature and its mysteries. There are so many natural wonders in this world, wonders that we would like to know more about... wonders that trigger our curiosity, wonders that open doors to the most exhilarating creations of nature. We can explore, we can do limitless things, but we must never forget that nature is unpredictable and we can't go against it, or manipulate it. Nature is stronger than all of us together. It is full of unexpected surprises and sometimes rebels against man. Everything we do in life–whether it's cycling, racing, swimming, scuba diving, boating, camping–everything has its dangers!"

He paused, and then added, "but...life goes on...doesn't it?"

Today, because of these remarkable explorations led by Norman, Thalia and the crew, the government not only preserves the Camuy Caves, but has transformed them into an important educational ecological attraction.

✷✸✷

I. Response Journal

After reading the story you will work with the Response Journal Questions. Share your answers in small groups. Each group will select one question and discuss the responses with the class.

1. How did the tragedy in the story affect you? Did you expect anything like that to happen? Explain your answer.

_____

_____

_____

_____

2. What do you think about the way the tragedy was dealt with by the crew?

_____

_____

_____

_____

3. Have you ever heard about a similar kind of tragedy? Write about it.

_____

_____

_____

_____

4. What would you have done when the water level rose if you had been the leader of the expedition?

_____

_____

_____

_____

_____

5. What do you think about what Nestor did? What were his motives? Would you have done the same?

_____

_____

_____

_____

_____

II. Mapping the Story

Use the chart below to map out the story. Show how in each part of the plot different elements are used to create the atmosphere related to the genre. In groups of three, compare and discuss the story map. In whole-class discussion, come to a consensus for each item on the chart.

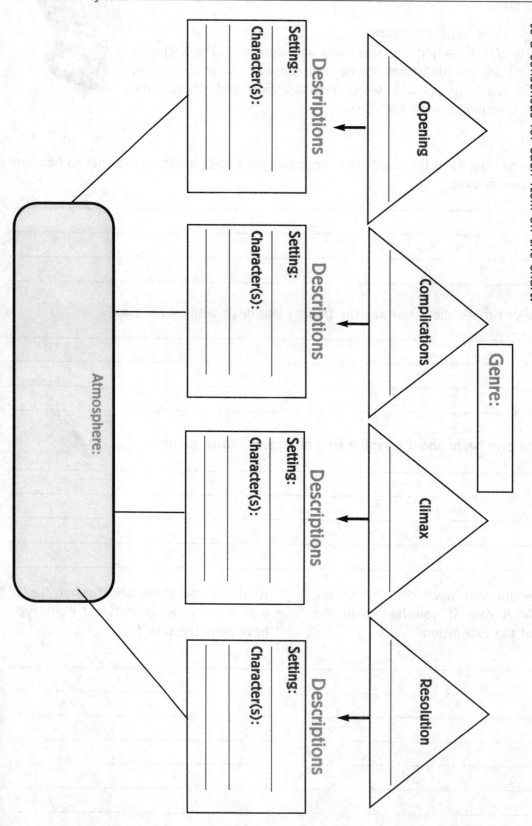

Genre:

Opening

Descriptions

Character(s):

Setting:

Complications

Descriptions

Character(s):

Setting:

Climax

Descriptions

Character(s):

Setting:

Resolution

Descriptions

Character(s):

Setting:

Atmosphere:

III. Comprehension Questions

1. Where are the caves located in Puerto Rico?

_____

_____

_____

2. Who is Norman Veve?

_____

_____

_____

3. What is speleology?

_____

_____

_____

4. In what year did this story take place?

_____

_____

_____

5. What is the name of the cave they were exploring?

_____

_____

_____

6. Who is Thalia?

_____

_____

_____

7. Why did Thalia take a measuring device to these explorations?

_____

_____

_____

8. What happened during the expedition that was unexpected?

_____

_____

_____

IV. Looking More Closely

1. Skim through the story to determine if there were any mistakes made in this expedition. Compare your answers with your classmates.

_____

_____

_____

_____

V. Reflecting Further on the Story

Work with a partner. Be prepared to discuss your answers with the class.

1. What are some of the problems you might encounter while in a cave?

_____

_____

_____

2. Is there a sport you would like to try but are afraid of doing so? Explain why you are afraid.

_____

_____

_____

3. Have you ever been to a cave? Which one and where?

_____

_____

_____

4. Why do you think the preservation of caves is important?

_____

_____

_____

VI. Springboard

Going Beyond

Find an article about an expedition, exploration or a similar activity.
National Geographic Magazine could be a source of information for this activity.
Narrate the event in detail to the class and point out the dangers that were encountered.

Researching the Topic

1. Find information about:
   - The Amazon Forest
   - Paulo Paiakan from Brazil
   - What happened to the Indians in Brazil when the government began the construction of the longest highway in the world.
2. Find information on some of the recent natural disasters brought about by the phenomenon of El Niño. Analyze the information you find to determine if the force of nature is rebelling against man's manipulation of the environment. Find a newspaper or magazine article and report on some of the latest incidents to the class.

_____

_____

_____

3. Why do you think natural disasters occur? Present the reasons for your opinion. Are there ways of preventing natural disasters?

_____

_____

_____

4. Find information and discuss in class your findings on one of the personalities mentioned below.
   a. Jacques Cousteau, marine biologist
   b. Carl Walenda, circus performer

13. School Blues

Searching for information

Ask your parents or grandparents what school was like for them. Work with a partner. First, talk about how education has changed. Then fill in the chart below.

EDUCATION

Past	Present
_____	_____
_____	_____
_____	_____
_____	_____
_____	_____
_____	_____
_____	_____

Brainstorming

Brainstorm about the ideal school today. Write down your ideas.

_____

_____

_____

_____

_____

_____

Guide Questions

Take a few minutes to study the questions below. Be prepared to discuss them.

- What is your opinion about schools today?
- Do you think too much homework is assigned?
- What is a good teacher?
- How much time do you think should be devoted to studying?

Reflective Writing

1. Think about your elementary school days and choose two of the questions below to write about. You will read your paper to the class.

   - How was your experience in elementary school?
   - Talk about your favorite teacher and one you disliked.

     How were they different?
   - Were you able to play and have fun when you were young or did you feel overburdened by homework?

   _____

   _____

   _____

   _____

   _____

2. Think about what education should be like today. Write a description of the type of school that would be ideal. Include the courses students should take and the activities a school should offer. Use the ideas you jotted down in "Searching for Information"

   _____

   _____

   _____

   _____

   _____

School Blues: Kids Hate Them, Moms Too!

Terry Mezo

"Monday Blues" some mothers call it, because the hectic weekly routine begins. I call it "weekly blues." It begins early Monday morning and continues every day of the week. I start by waking the girls up, and they start fighting for their turn to use the bathroom. I try to get my youngest child to open his eyes, but I end up dressing him while he is still asleep. Then my shouting begins. "Hurry... hurry! We´re running late like always! Get your shoes on. Comb your hair. Did you eat something? What are you waiting for? Aren´t you girls old enough to get some Wheat Flakes or Fruit Circles in a bowl, for crying out loud! Move it. Move it!" My shouting continues, "I´m getting pretty annoyed already." Simultaneously, I´m getting ready for my job and I´m hoping I don´t forget anything important.

I don´t get a chance to have any breakfast. I rush to work, put in my day´s work and I rush home to get that meal on the stove before I pick up the kids. For some reason, it seems as if the kids are on a crash diet all day! By 2:30 I´ve got to be in front of that school gate or they will have a heart attack thinking I´ve forgotten them. This is the time of the day that I dread the most, not because I´m picking up my kids, but because all hell starts breaking loose.

Once inside the car, my daily lecture begins. "What is the first thing you kids are going to do when we get home?" I ask.

Everyone shouts as if they were rehearsing a song. "Take our uniforms off, put them away, and take a bath!"

I am waiting for the next question, "Mom, what did you cook?"

"Spaghetti," I answer.

Vivi says, "Yummy!"

Ariane says, "Oh Mom, why did you cook that? Can you make some mashed potatoes for me?"

"No," I reply. "That´s what we are having for dinner. What do you kids think, that I´m some kind of maid?"

I park the car and give each one the book bags, those extremely heavy schoolbags which can easily fracture anyone´s vertebrae! Each one weighs approximately forty to fifty-five pounds and my son barely weighs thirty-eight pounds. In we go, and while the children take their baths, I check twenty-seven notebooks. There are nine notebooks per child, and I set aside all the ones that contain homework, announce tests, and dictations. The lists of homework they´ve been given can be compared to any college student´s work.

Hysteria begins! My daughter´s math teacher assigns thirty-five problems, not ten but thirty-five.

I am a teacher too, and I wonder if these teachers have any children. "No, they must be single," I tell myself. I wonder what they do when they get home... I imagine each of them picking up an entertaining magazine and browsing through it. If they were good teachers, they would know that ten exercises can work more miracles than thirty-five. The other day Vivi started at 4:00 p.m. and finished at 8:22 p.m. She was exhausted, and I would have had some choice words for her teacher if I had bumped into her that very moment. My second-grade daughter has to study for a test. Since I am monitoring all this torture, I read the criteria for the test. Students must be able to define the following concepts: *metaphor*, *simile* and *onomatopoeia*. This was enough to get me hysterical. My first-grade son is asked to explain, not identify, the kinds of sentences: imperative, exclamation, and interrogative. I was so mad I pinched myself and couldn´t feel it!

What are we doing to these kids? Do we want to have mentally and emotionally happy children? Must they read fluently and write perfectly in pre-kinder? Does the Department of Education supervise what goes on in schools, both private and public? Does the curriculum meet the real needs of our students? Is this curriculum realistic? Need our children be bombarded with all this nonsense at such early stages? Life is going to be challenging enough as it is already. They are going to have to work hard, very hard. Must they start this struggle at such a tender age? I am sure I´m not the only parent going through this daily struggle.

It is amazing how people will gather in protest when it´s time to save the planet, or to save the whales. Hey parents! Wake up! Save our children from this insanity. Let´s let them sing, play, dance and live happily. Let´s teach them a poem and let them find the beauty in it. Let´s give them time to be creative, sociable and helpful. Let´s let them ride bikes and roller blades. Let´s read an enjoyable story that gives them good examples of morals, ethics and love. They will inevitably grow up whether we like it or not, and I, for one, feel sad because they will not have what I did: time to be a kid and enjoy life!

I can still remember those days when my mom used to say, "Okay kids, get ready for bedtime. There is school tomorrow." I´d jump into bed and wait for everyone to be sound asleep, and jump right up and put on my uniform and my shoes. That way all I had to do the next day was get up, brush my teeth and be on my way, because I was eager to get to school. The morning walk to school along with all the other kids from the neighborhood was so joyful. Going to school was something that all—or at least most— children enjoyed.

A day at school was one of fun in which not only learning took place, but many other activities that made us grow closer as human beings. It was a place where stress was hardly felt, and where we were all eager to think and willing to create by using our imagination.

Many mornings classes began with music. Our teacher would bring in music from other countries so that we could appreciate the instruments other people played. After this, we would all stand up and learn a little about the folk dances of these countries and try them out ourselves. It was so much fun! The teacher would bring in pictures for us to see the special clothing they wore. Other times he would bring different instruments for us to play. We weren´t musicians, but we felt great satisfaction because somehow our teacher managed to make it sound beautiful.

We would then take an art class. It was amazing how many things we learned to do. We learned sewing, different kinds of crafts, knitting, embroidery, cooking, and fixing and setting up things. All the students were very creative and happy. The word "stress" did not exist; kids did not suffer from such a thing. This only happened to grown-ups.

Once classes were over we would end the schoolday with the walk back home. We walked and chatted about all the events that had taken place during the day, and then we would go home and play because homework was not what it is today. I don´t recall ever having to jam tons of illogical things into my brain. We did a couple of school tasks and we had the rest of the afternoon to play. T.V. was not at the top of the entertainment list. Most kids were outdoors running in the streets, playing catch, baseball, jacks, jumping rope, roller skating, riding bicycles, or sometimes just walking along the countryside.

The road was so peaceful and lovely. There were trees on both sides which gave shade to the entire place as if you were walking through a tunnel covered by a tightly knitted canopy. When you looked to your right, you could see the sugarcane fields that extended to the very lap of a hill. As we strolled along, we told stories and jokes, and occasionally we would stop and pick up the tiny *jobillo* fruit that had fallen from the trees. Further ahead we´d find some *tamarindos*. When we got to the bridge, we´d sit there for a while and enjoy the water running under our feet. Some of the guys would take off their pants and dive into the water in underwear. We would laugh so hard. Sometimes we´d walk along the brook and pick up some *camándula* beads to make some attractive necklaces after we got home.

Other times Toguicho, an old man from the neighborhood, would bring out his old horse and his wooden wagon. We would all climb in and the poor horse had a lot of pulling to do. We´d ride up to the sugarcane fields and Toguicho would peel some sugar-cane for us with his very sharp machete, and that would quiet us down for a long while. We would just sit there sucking away, making sure that not one drop of that cane would go to waste. And when the *quenepa* season began, we waited for Pellón to get someone to climb that gigantic tree and throw those sweet, juicy seeds to the ground. I just loved them!

Remembering, I think about how quickly it all went by and how unfortunate my kids are because they will never walk on Las Flores Street, that once shady canopy. The trees have now been cut down and substituted by a highway that leads to the next town. They will not suck on that sweet sugarcane that grew so close to the house. Villa Polilla is now built over the sugarcane valley. This development made of wood earned its name because people knew that the termites or *polillas* would eventually destroy the homes. And they were right! Today many people have rebuilt their homes, but have used con-crete instead. Toguicho and his horse are both gone. Pellón is not there anymore. The *quenepas* go to waste, since there´s no one to climb the trees and pick them. The kids no longer walk to or from school. Parents have to drop them off and pick them up. Kids don´t play in the afternoons. There´s too much homework to be done. If there´s any time left at all they sit at home in front of that hypnotic eye or worse than that, they sit in front of their addictive Super Nintendos, killing and fighting and watching the "virtu-al reality" of life as part of their weekly blues.

I. Response Journal

After reading the editorial, work with the Response Journal Questions. Share your answers in small groups. Each group will select one question and discuss the responses with the class.

1. What came to your mind when you read the title "School Blues"?

_____

_____

_____

_____

2. How did you feel as you were reading the editorial? Were you able to identify with the author's feelings?

_____

_____

_____

_____

3. Do you know any family similar to the one in the editorial?

_____

_____

_____

_____

4. Write about some of your fondest memories of elementary school. How much do you think you learned?

_____

_____

_____

_____

_____

5. Write about what you liked least about elementary school.

_____

_____

_____

_____

_____

II. Mapping the Editorial

Use the chart below to map out the editorial. Show how the elements on the map help to develop the theme. In groups of three, compare and discuss the map. Talk about how the genre affects the reading. In whole-class discussion, come to a consensus for each item on the chart.

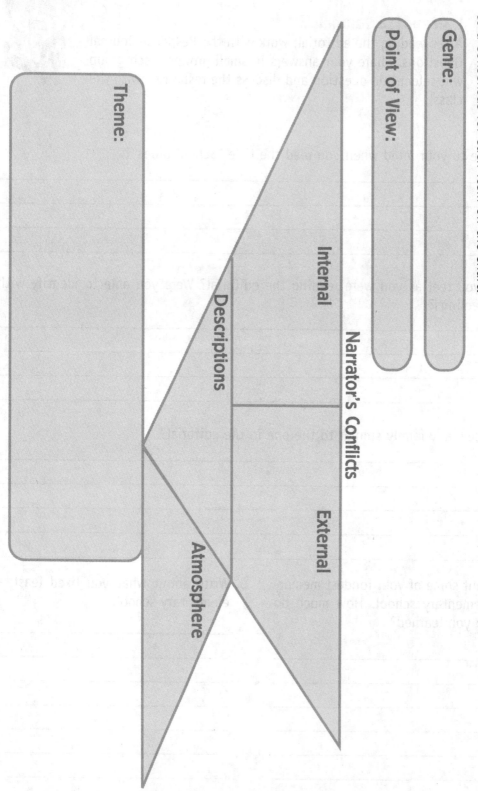

Genre:

Point of View:

Narrator's Conflicts

Internal

External

Descriptions

Atmosphere

Theme:

III. Comprehension Questions
Work with a partner. Answer the questions and be prepared to discuss your answers.

1. Why do some people call Mondays "blue"?

_____

_____

2. What happens every Monday morning at the narrator's home?

_____

_____

_____

3. What is the mother's routine after 2:30 p.m.?

_____

_____

4. How was school in her days?

_____

_____

_____

5. Why did she feel her school days were better?

_____

_____

_____

6. Who was Toguicho?

_____

_____

_____

7. What did the kids do after school?

_____

_____

_____

IV Looking More Closely

1. What are children's attitudes towards school nowadays?

_____

_____

_____

_____

2. What is ironical about this editorial in terms of teachers in the past and teachers today?

_____

_____

_____

_____

3. Who is unhappy, the kids, the mom or both?

_____

_____

_____

_____

_____

4. What method of development does the narrator use? How does she help you understand what she feels about education?

_____

_____

_____

_____

5. Did you ever do any of the things the mother did as a child?

_____

_____

_____

_____

V. Reflecting Further on the Editorial

Working on your own, answer the following questions. Discuss your answers with the class.

1. What part of the editorial did you like best?

_____

_____

_____

2. Are the present and past situations that the narrator describes realistic or unrealistic? Explain.

_____

_____

_____

_____

3. List the characteristics of a good teacher in the spaces provided below.

_____ _____

_____ _____

_____ _____

_____ _____

Write a paragraph defining what a good teacher is, using the characteristics you listed. Read it to the class.

_____

_____

_____

_____

4. When do you categorize a teacher as bad? Explain.

_____

_____

_____

_____

VI. Springboard
Exploring

Work with a partner. Choose one of the questions below, answer it and be prepared to discuss it with your classmates.

1. If you analyze the environment presented in the editorial, can it be compared to our environment today? What are the similarities or differences?

_____

_____

_____

2. Find and list the clues from the reading that helped you put the narrator's story into a time frame?

_____

_____

_____

3. Write a description of the fruit mentioned in the story.

_____

_____

_____

4. Make a chart that illustrates the forms of entertainment for children in the past and the present based on the editorial.

Entertainment Yesterday	Entertainment Today

5. Think about the increase in crime and other social problems in the world today. Write about how these are affecting families in terms of entertainment.

_____

_____

_____

_____

_____

6. Write a description of a perfect family.

_____

_____

_____

_____

_____

Contrasting Times

Work together in groups of four or five students. Create a poster board that illustrates what life was like twenty years ago and what it is like today. You can use magazines and newspapers. You will need scissors, glue and magic markers. Some of the areas you can illustrate are: music, games, clothing styles, children's attitudes, parents, socializing, entertainment, food, transportation, communication and others.

14. A Fallen Star

Brainstorming

Make a list of words that come to your mind after you read the title.

_____   _____
_____   _____
_____   _____
_____   _____
_____   _____
_____   _____
_____   _____

Make Your Prediction

What do you think the story is going to be about?

_____

_____

_____

_____

A Fallen Star

Terry Mezo

We had heard the rumor about the girl from our mother. Since we didn't know exactly when she was going to come, we changed our usual chatting spot to the front of the house.

Perry and I were standing outside the gate on the sidewalk when we saw our neighbors arrive with her. This was going to be her new home. We couldn't control our curiosity and stared directly at her to get a closer look. She must have been as curious about us as we were about her because we realized she was reciprocating our glance. She was about seven or eight years old. She had short blonde hair and clear green eyes. Her triangle shaped face was peculiar, yet she had an adorable smile and the effect was very pleasant. She seemed rather shy. Her simple dress accentuated her thin body.

Perry and I were a couple of years older than her. Perry was telling me that he had heard more details about the new kid on the block... "She was lost in a park in Texas. The police were never able to locate her mom or her dad so she was taken to a parish in Alamo, and the priest there was a good friend of the Cetty family. The priest knew this couple was unable to have children and soon sent them news about adding a member to their family."

I was rather intrigued because our neighbors were so strange, unfriendly and secretive about everything. They never sat on their balcony and they certainly didn't like kids. I say this because I remember the time the old man was upset at Perry and me because we snatched some *acerolas* from his tree. The man was furious at us, but the caribbean cherries looked so temping–so red, big, and ripe. We were savoring them before we even picked them! We just had to go for them. Anyway, they never picked them and they would spoil right on the tree. Mom scolded me so badly for stealing *acerolas* and prohibited me to go near that tree ever again. I tried not to even look that way until the day the little girl arrived.

There were lots of kids in our neighborhood. We played hide and seek just about every afternoon while Nelly watched us through the fence. She looked as if she were in prison. Perry and I approached her to make conversation many times. She wanted to come out and play but they wouldn't allow her to. Sometimes, after fifteen minutes of chatting with us through the fence, they would call her inside. We felt compassion for her. Our first conversation was really a cross-examination. We asked her if it was true that she had been lost. She confirmed that it was.

Two days after her arrival she was registered in school. We were able to walk to and from school with her and get to know her better. Once, I asked, "Nelly, are you happy in your new home?"

She replied, "It's okay, but they make me do a lot of work. I feel like a slave sometimes."

"Don't feel like that. My mother makes me do housework, too," I remarked.

Time passed quickly and she had adjusted. At least that's what Perry and I thought. Soon Nelly had turned twelve years old. She was blossoming into quite a beautiful swan, and we were witnesses to that. Even my brother felt attracted to her.

A few months after, my instincts told me things were not all that great. There was a sadness in her eyes that gave her unhappiness away. After school, I did my house chores rapidly and called her to the fence. "If you ever need my help, count on me. I am your friend," I said.

Tears came to her eyes as she said, "I don't know why these people wanted to have me. This man who wants to be my dad is strange. He hits me hard with a stick, and he tells me nasty things. They are always fighting. I think he believes in black magic."

"WHAT?" I couldn't contain myself. My mouth was wide open!

"Yes, it's true! You have to come over and help me open his bedroom door. It's always closed and I'm not allowed to go in."

"Tomorrow when we get home from school I'll go to your house."

The following day as soon as I got home I sneaked to her house. Her parents were still working. The door to her dad's room was locked, but there was a square space at the top of the door. She didn't have a ladder, and there was no way of reaching that height without a chair.

"I've got an idea," I said. "Climb onto the chair. Then stand on my shoulders and go in through that hole up there."

"Okay," she answered. She was very light and soon she had reached the hole above the door. While up there, she uttered, "Now I have another problem."

"What?" I inquired.

"Well, how am I supposed to land on the other side of the door? On my head?"

"Oh dear! We better think fast. We're gonna get caught," I said.

"Okay, I'll try to twist myself around," and so she did and landed on her feet. As she jumped I heard a loud thump followed by "Ouch!" and the door opened.

We made a quick detective search. We felt like Inspector Gadget! We found pictures of her and her mother inside these strange bottles. We opened the second drawer and at the bottom found a pile of pictures with big black X's on Nelly's face as well as on her mom's. Some strange prayers and mysterious artifacts were also found. We tried to leave no trace of our search.

"Quick, let's take all this junk and throw it away. This man believes in witchcraft." We gathered everything and called Perry to help us sneak all the paraphernalia out of the house.

When Perry got to the house, he thought our findings were hilarious. "What's going on?" he kept asking. "Oh! Wow! This man is a witch! He must have put a curse on you guys. Let's get rid of this and the curse will vanish."

Suddenly, we couldn't stop giggling. We felt like CIA agents. We were upset but excited at the same time. "Hurry, hurry, check if anyone is out on the street. We need a black bag," Perry said.

"Okay," I replied, "everything is settled."

During the next two weeks we didn't see Nelly. They drove her to school and picked her up from school. She sent me a note with my brother who was in her class. The note said, "My mom confronted my dad. They had a big argument. They are getting separated. He is leaving the house. Mom says he is weird and crazy."

"WOW!" I said to myself. "This sounds like a mystery movie." Perry and I were intrigued by the mystery that was unfolding in our neighborhood. We knew the inside story.

Some time later the man left his home. Nelly and her mom seemed to be happier for a while. Her mom started socializing more with the neighbors, and we were able to grow closer as friends–Perry, Nelly and I.

Life is not a bowl of cherries! Into her adolescence, Nelly's deep curiosity to find her roots–her mom and her family–continued to grow within her soul. I couldn't understand why she allowed these thoughts to disturb her so much. She also started hanging out with the wrong crowd. Perry and I still chatted with her every evening. We really cared for her. We were slightly older and tried comforting her.

One afternoon while I was raking the leaves, she showed up. I looked into her red eyes and perceived something very strange. "What is wrong with you? Were you crying?" I asked.

"I just took some acid," she replied.

"What are you telling me?"

"Some guys gave me a piece of paper with some acid drops and I took one," she told me.

My heart sank and I said, "Why are you doing this? You are such a sweet, pretty, intelligent person. You have a mom that cares for you... I don't understand you!"

The following year Perry and I started college. Our encounters with Nelly were less frequent, but we still cared about her a lot! Shortly after the semester began, I was home one evening studying for a test when Perry rushed into the house in total hysteria. "Did you hear the news?" he asked.

"What news?" I inquired.

"Nelly killed a guy!"

"What? Stop joking Perry. I've got some studying to do," I answered seriously.

"I'm not joking. She was high on acid, got into a serious argument with a young man and pulled the trigger on him."

"Oh my!" Silence took over and my mind drifted to that time when Nelly had recently moved in and she was standing on the fence watching us play. She looked like a helpless prisoner behind the fence. And now she would be in prison for twenty years I was told. I felt an ache in my heart to think of her behind bars. Was it fate? Or was this a curse running through her veins?

Perry and I mention her often. We know she could have made better choices. There are moments when we reflect upon events of her life and accept the fact that people can be like stars. Some shine brighter, others higher, and still others fall.

I. Response Journal

After reading the story, work with the Response Journal Questions. Share your answers in small groups. Each group will select one question and discuss the responses with the class.

1. What do you think happened to Nelly's parents? How do you think she must have felt?

_____

_____

_____

_____

2. Do you know anyone who was adopted? How does the person feel about his/her biological parents?

_____

_____

_____

_____

3. Why do you think Nelly got into drugs? Tell the group about someone you've heard of who takes drugs.

_____

_____

_____

_____

4. Do you think the drugs caused her to commit the murder? Explain.

_____

_____

_____

_____

_____

_____

5. How realistic do you think the story is?

_____

_____

_____

_____

_____

_____

II. Mapping the Story

Use the chart below to map out the story. Show how we find out about both the main and secondary characters through direct description and through their actions, words and reactions of the other characters. How does the characterization lead to the climax and resolution? In groups of three, compare and discuss the story map. Talk about how the genre affects the reading. In whole-class discussion, come to a consensus for each item on the chart.

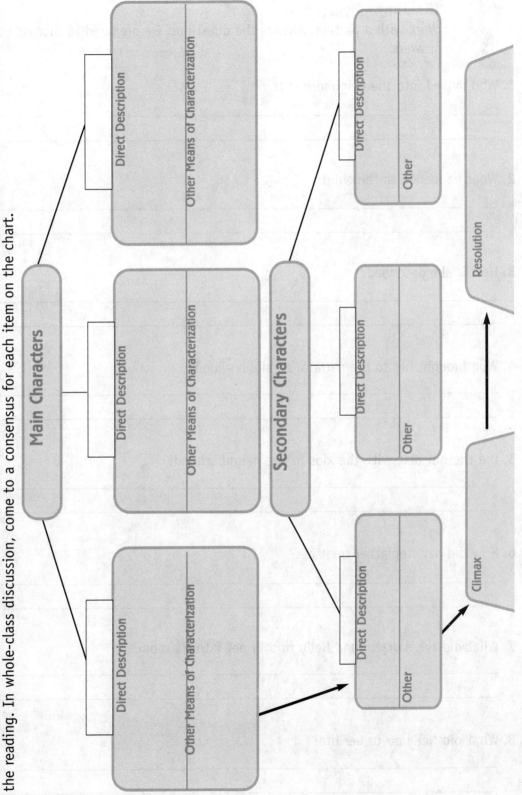

III. Comprehension Questions
Work with a partner. Answer the questions. Be prepared to discuss your answers.

1. Who moved into the neighborhood?

_____

_____

2. What happened to the child?

_____

_____

3. How is she described?

_____

_____

4. Who brought her to the narrator's neighborhood?

_____

_____

5. Did the girl play with the kids in the neighborhood?

_____

_____

6. How did her stepfather treat her?

_____

_____

7. What did the narrator and Nelly find in her father's room?

_____

_____

8. What did Nelly do to her life?

_____

_____

IV. Looking More Closely

1. What do you consider was Nelly's biggest mistake?

_____

_____

_____

2. What would you have done if you were in Nelly's situation?

_____

_____

_____

3. What advice would you give Nelly?

_____

_____

_____

4. What other choices did Nelly have? Explain.

_____

_____

_____

5. How is the title related to the content of the story?

_____

_____

_____

6. What is the main idea in the story?

_____

_____

_____

7. Do you think Nelly's destiny was already decided?

_____

_____

8. Do you think there is more than one conflict in the story? Explain.

_____

_____

_____

V. Reflecting Further on the Story

With a partner, choose two items from below to work with and discuss your answers with the class.

1. Because of the circumstances of her life, Nelly has to face a number of obstacles. List four of these obstacles and what you perceive to be the effects of them on her.

a. Obstacle _____

   Effect _____

b. Obstacle _____

   Effect _____

c. Obstacle _____

   Effect _____

d. Obstacle _____

   Effect _____

2. How complete is the characterization in the story? What additional information might you include to give more insight into the characters?

_____

_____

_____

_____

3. At the end of the story the narrator says that she and Perry often mention Nelly. What do you think they say when they talk about her?

_____

_____

_____

4. What kind of prisoner do you think Nelly was? What do you think will happen to her after she leaves prison?

_____

_____

_____

5. Do you think there is any hope for a person like Nelly? Why? Why not? As a prison warden, what kind of program would you recommend for her?

_____

_____

_____

6. How do you think the story would be different if Nelly or Perry had narrated it?

_____

_____

_____

VI. Springboard
Collaborative Activity

With a partner, make a questionnaire to find out people's opinions about one of the issues presented in the story. Interview three to five people each. Present your findings to the class orally.

Issues: Child Abandonment   Drug Abuse
       Child Abuse   Black Magic
       Adoption   Heredity vs. Environment
       The Penal System

Going Beyond

Confronting Obstacles- Look for a newspaper or magazine article about someone dealing with one of the problems mentioned in the story. Summarize the article, find the main idea(s) and present it to the class.

Researching the Topic and Presenting Your Views

Find an article related to a form of drug abuse. You can use magazines, newspapers, professional journals or the Internet.

Summarize the article orally in class. Focus on the kind of drug abuse and the treatment for it. Keep in mind that alcohol abuse and smoking are two kinds of drug abuse.

Take a Stand (Debate)
Should drugs be legalized? The teacher will divide the class into two groups—one in favor of the legalization of drugs and the other against it. With the classmates in your group, fill in the appropriate list below. Working together, develop your opening statement with your group's view and your arguments for your position. Have a debate.

Reasons for Legalization   Reasons Against Legalization

_____   _____
_____   _____
_____   _____
_____   _____
_____   _____
_____   _____
_____   _____
_____   _____
_____   _____
_____   _____
_____   _____

Vocabulary Builder

Use this chart to enter new vocabulary words and their definitions.

1. *Life Rhythms*

_____
_____
_____
_____
_____
_____

2. *The Caribbean Pearl*

_____
_____
_____
_____
_____

3. Panas

_____
_____
_____
_____

4. *A Virtual World*

_____
_____
_____
_____

5. *Mo-der*

_____
_____
_____

6. *An Angel in My Path*

_____
_____
_____
_____
_____

7. *Virtuoso*

_____
_____
_____
_____
_____

8. *Lumpy Soup*

_____
_____
_____
_____

9. *The Latin Alien*

_____
_____
_____
_____

10. *The Menorah*

_____
_____
_____
_____

11. *Falling*

_____
_____
_____
_____
_____
_____

12. *The* Camuy *Caves*

_____
_____
_____
_____
_____
_____

13. *School Blues*

_____
_____
_____
_____
_____
_____

14. *A Fallen Star*

_____
_____
_____
_____
_____
_____